AF269059

HARASS DATING

Harass Dating

Anthony Goluszek

Copyright © 2019 by Anthony Goluszek.

Library of Congress Control Number: 2019912894

PAPERBACK: 978-1-951461-13-3
EBOOK: 978-1-951461-14-0

All rights reserved. No part of this publication may be reproduced, distributed, or transmitted in any form or by any electronic or mechanical means, without the prior written permission of the publisher, except in the case of brief quotations embodied in critical reviews and certain other noncommercial uses permitted by copyright law.

Ordering Information:

For orders and inquiries, please contact:
1-888-404-1388
www.goldtouchpress.com
book.orders@goldtouchpress.com

Printed in the United States of America

There is nothing more disheartening than seeing injustice in the workplace, especially when sexual harassment is involved. It is something which has happened time and time again throughout the years, but it never gets easier to hear the detailed wrongdoings of those who take advantage of others and harass them until they feel completely at a loss of what to do. This feeling of helplessness only gets worse when those in charge fail to help their workers complaining of this harassment. We explore all of this and so much more in *Harass Dating* by author Anthony Goluszek.

Throughout this book, there are many documents detailing the harassment that Anthony Goluszek experienced at the hands of his co-workers during the late-70s to mid-80s. He worked as an electrician at H.P. Smith in Chicago and according to the court documents, felt as though he was targeted and harassed, and subsequently discharged from his position, due to both the harassment he complained of to his higher-ups as well as the fact he is Polish. Clearly, neither are valid reasons to discharge somebody and it is shameful to hear about the harassment he endured during these years of employment at H.P. Smith. To make matters worse, it seems as though his voice was never truly heard when he needed assistance most, resulting in years of court cases that ultimately didn't serve him the justice he so greatly deserved.

While I can honestly say it was troubling to read of his mistreatment while employed with H.P. Smith, I think it is commendable that the author was willing to put all of this information out there for the public so they can see what he dealt with and how it is despicable that he was not given proper justice in the end. It's an intriguing read that will surely leave you shocked and appalled at the actions of both his fellow workers as well as the way the courts handled his case.

It is unfortunate that anyone should have to go through what this author did and it is easy to see why it was an experience he hasn't forgotten all these years later. Even so, it is important that people speak up when this happens and when they feel as though they haven't been heard, it matters that they have another outlet to make their voice heard about the injustices they had to go through.

Make sure to pick up your copy of *Harass Dating* by Anthony Goluszek so you too can see sexual harassment from the male perspective. There is no doubting its importance in the modern workplace.

Certofocate

Tony Goluszek

FOR YOUR VERY OUTSTANDING
PERFORMANCE
YOU ARE AWARDED

"One Attaboy"

ONE THOUSAND "ATTABOYS" QUALIFIES YOU TO BE A
LEADER OF MEN

WORK OVERTIME WITH A SMILE, EXPLAIN ASSORTED
PROBLEMS

TO MANAGEMENT, AND BE LOOKED UPON AS A
LOCAL HERO.

NOTE ONE "AWSHIT" WIPES THE BOARD CLEAN
AND YOU HAVE TO START ALL OVER AGAIN

February 8, 1984

Mr. Anthony Goluszek
H. P. Smith

Dear Tony:

The grievance you first submitted for Step 2 consideration on February 7, 1984 was by your own statement reviewed by supervision and denied at Step 1 on January 26, 1984.

Given these times, the grievance has not been submitted within the time limits as outlined in Article 10 of the Current Working Agreement. Therefore, the matter you outlined cannot be accepted as a proper grievance and is being returned to you. However, you may feel free to discuss a problem you have with supervision, superintendent, etc.

Very truly yours,

John J. Mietlicki
Industrial Relations Manager

JJM:dlm

ac: W. Clemente
       M. R. Malloy
       J. L. Gibbons
       J. T. Webb A. Luna
       M. P. Trendle

                                                      June 21, 1984

Anthony Goluszek
1239 Vincennes
Chicago Heights, Illinois 60411

                                    Re: International Brotherhood
                                           of Teamsters, Chauffeurs,
                                           Warehousemen & Helpers
                                           of America, Local 714
                                           (H.P. Smith)
                                           Case 13-CB-10633

Dear Mr. Goluszek:

The above-captioned case charging a violation under Section 8 of the
National Labor Relations Act, as amended, has been carefully investigated
and considered.

From the investigation, the evidence does not show that the Union's failure
to timely process your grievance rose to the level of gross negligence or
that the Union otherwise violated its duty of fair representation in this
matter. Office and Professional Employees International Union, Local
No. 2, AFL-CIO, 268 NLRB No. 207, (1984). I am, therefore, refusing
to issue complaint herein.

Pursuant to the National Labor Relations Board Rules and Regulations,
Series 8, as amended, you may obtain a review of this action by filing
an appeal with the Acting General Counsel addressed to the Office of
Appeals, National Labor Relations Board, Washington, D. C. 20570, and
a copy with me. This appeal must contain a complete statement setting
forth the facts and reasons upon which it is based. The appeal must be
received by the Acting General Counsel in Washington, D. C., by the close
of business on July 5, 1984. Upon good cause shown, however, the Acting
General Counsel may grant special permission for a longer period within

which to file. Any request for extension of time must be submitted to the Office of Appeals in Washington, and a copy of any such request should be submitted to me.

If you file an appeal, please complete the notice forms I have enclosed with this letter and send one copy of the form to each of the other parties. Their names and addresses are listed below. The notice forms should be mailed at the same time you file the appeal, but mailing the notice forms does not relieve you of the necessity for filing the appeal itself with the Acting General Counsel and a copy of the appeal with the Regional Director within the time stated above.

Very truly yours,

Donald J. Crawford
Regional Director

Enclosure
Certified Mail
(Return Receipt Requested)
cc: See Page 2

IN THE UNITED STATES DISTRICT COURT FOR THE NORTHERN DISTRICT OF ILLINOIS EASTERN DIVISION

ANTHONY P. GOLUSZEK,	)	
	)	
	)	
Plaintiff,	)	
	)	No. 86 C 8412
v.	)	
	)	
H.P. SMITH,	)	
	)	
Defendant.	)	

MEMORANDUM OPINION AND ORDER

In this Title VII case, the Plaintiff Anthony Goluszek claims that he was the victim of sexual harassment by other males who worked for the defendant H.P. Smith. He also claims that H.P. Smith fired him because (1) he is Polish and (2) in retaliation for his complaining about the sexual harassment. In this opinion, the court addresses the merits of H.P. Smith's motion for summary judgment.

Facts[1]

Anthony Goluszek has never been married nor has he lived anywhere but at his mother's home. According to Goluszek's psychiatrist, Goluszek comes from an "unsophisticated background" and has led as "isolated existence" with "little or no sexual experience." Goluszek "blushes easily" and is abnormally sensitive to comments pertaining to sex. Plaintiff's Exhibit ("PX") A.

---

[1] The parties submitted their statements of uncontested and contested facts. N.D. Ill. Gen. R. 12. Pursuant to local rule and for purposes of the defendant's motion, the court treats as admitted any factual assertion not expressly controverted by the opposing party.

H.P. Smith is a division of James River Corporation engaged in the business of treating paper with a polyethylene coating for use as freezer wrap and the like. In December of 1976 H.P. Smith hired Goluszek as an electronic maintenance mechanic whose job was to maintain and repair the machines used in production. While he worked at H.P. smith, Goluszek was represented by Local 714 of the International Brotherhood of Teamsters[2] and his employment was governed by the union's collective bargaining agreement with H.P. Smith. A subsection of Section 11 of that agreement provides that an employee's "(w)illfully creating avoidable waste of time or material" constitutes a just cause for discharge. Goluszek Deposition Exhibit ("Dep. x.") 18a at 22.

Shortly after Golluszek started at H.P. Smith in December of 1976, a number of machine operators questioned him as to why he had no wife or girlfriend and joked that one had to be married to work there. One year later, the same operators told him that if he could not fix a machine, they would call his "daddy" in. Apparently the operators were referring to Goluszek's supervisor Michael Byczek who, like Goluszek, is of Polish descent. Goluszek reported the latter incident to his night supervisor Cal Adair. Adair responded by using the same remark the operators had used regarding Goluszek's "daddy." In 1978, Adair on one occasion told Goluszek that if Goluszek could not fix a machine he would be sent to a sausage factory. Adair also said Gollusze, needed to "get married and get some of that soft pink smelly stuff that's between the legs of a woman." Goluszek responded that Adair should not comment on Goluszek's personal life. PX B.

In the spring of 1979, certain operators told Goluszek he should get married and that he should go out with another employee named Kathy Kristen because she "fucks." Goluszek reported this to Adair whose response was that if Goluszek did not fix a machine they would get "Kathy Kristen to fix Tony." PX B.

---

2   Local 714 was originally a defendant in this action, but on January 7, 1988 pursuant to a stipulation the court dismissed all claims against the union with prejudice.

Sometime subsequently in 1979, H.P. Smith transferred Goluszek to the day shift. On a number of occasions on this shift, employees driving jeeps threatened to knock Goluszek off of his ladder. Goluszek complained about this practice to Byczek and to the General Manager John Van Buskirk. They assured him the matter would be investigated. Goluszek also filed a grievance with Local 714 which the union declined to pursue. He then sent a copy of his grievance to the National Labor Relations Broad which in turn directed him to the Occupational Safety and Health Commission. ("OSHA"). After an investigation, OSHA informed Goluszek by letter that it had found no violation and that H. P. Smith was observing appropriate safety measures.

On October 16, 1980, Plant Engineer J. R. Macfarlane issued a warning to Goluszek regarding Goluszek's careless installation of a ballast in a light fixture. Macfarlane warned that continued poor performance would lead to termination.

Subsequently Goluszek requested a meeting which was held on December 4, 1980. Plant Manager Jim Rooney and Byczek were present. Goluszek complained about the Macfarlene reprimand and the danger forklift drivers presented to him. He even threatened court action. A similar meeting was held with Van Buskirk and others on February 27, 1981. Van Buskirk later by letter informed Goluszek that his allegations were without substance and warned that "a continuation of actions on [Goluszek's] part which result in personal unrest, employee antagonism, wasteage of company material or time, is sufficient cause for [Goluszek's] termination." Goluszek Dep. X. 10.

H.P. Smith transferred Goluszek back to the night shift sometime in 1981. On that shift, the operators periodically asked Goluszek if he had gotten any "pussy" or had oral sex, showed him pictures of nude women, told him they would get him "fucked," accused him of being gay or bisexual, and made other sex-related comments. The operators also poked him in the buttocks with a stick. Goluszek complained to General Foreman Bill Clements about the remarks, but Clemente did nothing. Goluszek has admitted that the employees on both shifts talked about sex with one another and used words such as "fuck" in those conversations. He also admits that comments about sex were made that were not directed at him. E.G., Goluszek Dep. at 191-95.

In 1983 and 1984, a number of complaints arose regarding Goluszek's job performance. In May of 1983, Production Foreman Leo Karpinsky (who also is Polish) issued a verbal warning to Goluszek because of Goluszek's failure to follow safety procedures and use protective sleeves. As a consequence of his neglect, Goluszek had been burned when working on a defective heater. On January 18, 1984, Karpinski gave Goluszek a written warning for wasting time by being out of the plant without permission on January 12, 1984.[3] Also in January of 1984 employee Roy Goytia complained to Clemente that Goluszek had been trying to get Goytia to complain about Karpinski. On January 26, 1984, Clemente spoke with Goluszek and Goytia at which time Goluszek complained that he was being harassed by employees "out there talking to me about butt fucking in the ass." Goluszek Dep. at Clemente told Goluszek such statements were mere "shop talk." After Goluszek filed a grievance against Clemente, Clemente apologized. The grievance was eventually denied as untimely.

Goluszek's problems continued in April of 1984. On April 10, 1984, Goluszek received a warning for excessive tardiness, his third in three years. On April 11, 1984, Clemente and Karpinski found Goluszek with his feet up on the desk when he was supposed to be looking for a part. H.P. Smith suspended Goluszek for three days and warned that a similar incident would result in termination. Goluszek filed a grievance regarding the April 11 incident, but that grievance was dismissed when he failed to appear at the grievance meeting.

May of 1984 marked the end of Goluszek's employment with H.P. Smith. On May 8, 1984, Clemente issued him another written warning for being late four times in the prior twenty-seven days. On May 9, 1984, Goluszek took six hours to complete a project that normally took one to two.[4] On May 10, 1984, Goluszek admitted that he had not done any work for one and one-half hours. On May 14, 1984, Goluszek was absent from work without an excuse. The next day Goluszek again did

---

3   Goluszek appears to believe that Karpinski filed the warning because Goluszek had filed a safety report against Karpinski regarding the latter's procedure for repairing a broken water hose. <u>See</u> PX C.

4   Goluszek attributes the delay to his difficulty in finding a part. <u>See</u> PX C.

    ANTHONY GOLUSZEK

nothing for an hour and a half despite being given a work order. Goluszek claims to have been looking for the requisite tools. On May 16, 1984, H.P. Smith suspended Goluszek indefinitely. Eventually H.P. Smith fired Goluszek and Goluszek's grievance was denied. Goluszek admits that the company followed its progressive discipline policy before subjecting him to discharge.

On April 21, 1984, H.P. Smith fired a Hispanic employee named Tony Luna for the same reason it fired Goluszek – willfully creating avoidable waste of time or material. But unlike Goluszek, Luna prior to his discharge had never been issued a three-day suspension or a final warning that further misconduct would be cause for discharge. H.P. Smith also failed to give Luna a chance to explain his actions. On May 21, 1984, H.P. Smith reinstated Luna.

Finally, some evidence exists that H.P. Smith reacted differently to female claims of sexual harassment than male claims. In a letter dated November 29, 1972, an H.P. Smith supervisor warned an employee regarding the latter's "harassing of a female employee." The letter warned that further harassment would lead to disciplinary action or even discharge. PX E.

Law Offices
CLAUDIA ONEY, P.C.

EAST MONROE STREET • SUITE 3420 • CHICAGO, ILLINOIS
60603 • 312-782-1964

January 17, 1989

Mr. Anthony Goluszek
1239 Vincennes Ave.
Chicago Heights, Illinois 60411

Re: Goluszek vs. H.P. Smith

Dear Tony:

As I discussed with you in my office, the judge's ruling in your case was based on her finding that your termination was not due to your complaints of harassment. In other words, the judge found that your discharge was not in retaliation for you making complaints of harassment.

As such, this ruling did not hold that you were not sexually harassed. In fact, the judge described the working conditions under which you worked to be very difficult. She did not contest your testimony of harassment. She simply ruled that even though you may have been harassed, this harassment was not the cause of your discharge.

As you know, the question of whether you are protected under Title VII from the harassment you experienced was not part of the trial, since the judge had earlier ruled that you are not so protected. This is the primary basis on which an appeal would be filed. If the appeals court finds that you are so protected, your case will be remanded for trial on that issue. In that event, a trial will be held where the question of the harassment itself will be litigated. In view of the court's finding of the harassing atmosphere at H.P. Smith, a certain amount of that issue has already been shown. In short, the question is not so much whether you were harassed, but whether you are protected under Title VII from this harassment. That is what appealing your case would answer.

Finally, we had discussed appealing your case and the method of payment in that event. I still await your decision on whether you wish to appeal. Specifically, $2,000.00 payable by March 1, 1989 and $1,500,00 payable by January 1, 1990. These amounts include a petition for hearing by the U.S. Supreme Court if we lose in the Seventh Circuit Court of Appeals. If the U.S. Supreme Court agrees to hear your case we would discuss the fees for that level of appeal when so notified. Your chances of having the case heard by the U.S. Supreme Court are no better than about one in sixteen. Please be aware that a notice of appeal should be filed no later than January 23, 1989.

I also want to thank you for your cooperation and assistance throughout the trial. And, although your sister did not testify I also appreciate her help. I will be waiting for our direction as to whether or not to order the transcripts of Mr. Tony Luna's testimony, Mr. Emil Bohacz's testimony, Mr. Casey Kubeckio's testimony and Mr. John Mietlicki's testimony. These witnesses were valuable in establishing the atmosphere of harassment at H.P. Smith. Mr. Bohacz and Mr. Kubecki, in particular will be helpful if we proceed on appeal sicne they described being sexually harassed by the company. Mr. Luna and Mr. Mietlicki discribed harassing people sexually so that their testimony will be used by us as well. Again, we will ask the appellate court to find the trial judge to have erred in finding that males cannot harass males under Title VII.

Sincerely,
CLAUDIA ONEY, ESQ.

Claudia Oney

CC/jll

cc:

1239 Vincennes Ave.
Chicago Hts., IL 60411
(312) 755-6493

Dear Sirs:

My sexual harassment case was judged by Judge Ann Williams of U.S. District Court, Everett McKinley Dirken Biulding, Chgo., IL. My lawyers name was Claudia Oney, 55 E. Monroe St., Ste. number 3520 Chgo., IL. 60603. My file and docket number is 8608412.

My original complaint was at the Judicial Inquiry Board, they refered me to you for complaints against federal judges.

My complaint is that the judge in her summary decision was that only women can be sexually harassed not men.

I had three witnesse's that testified in court, Casy Kubicki, Emil Bohas knew of the harassment I was going through. Anthony Luna, my union stewart even knew of harassment and even me being assaulted with a stick while working.

I was rejected help from my Union 714 and all of company management of H.P.

Smith, and being disciplined while it was going on making the charge of retaliation.

I told the judged by letter, before going to court that I was getting bad references for work which gave me no money to pay for appeals in seveth district court. I got all kinds of job rejecting letters

I gave as evidence all kinds of letters verifing my complaining. This company was so bad I had to take valium medication while I was working on the job. I recieved all kinds of threating letters to put up with all kinds of harassment or I would be fired. The company's own memorandum introduced, into evidence of court, tells of there being bad supervisors reputation in June of 1984.

I feel that the judges ruling was so bad to state she a pervert or was paid off. I know if I was on the streets with this sexual harassment talk that I would be arrested and put away or worse. She makes this misconduct acceptable there by making the charge of Federal Judges misconduct complaint. Thank you.

Sincerely,

Anthony P. Goluszek

United States Court of Appeals

For the Seventh Circuit
Chicago, Illinois 60604
January 30, 1991

Before

Hon.   RICHARD A. POSNER, Circuit Judge

Hon.   JOEL M. FLAUM, Circuit Judge

Hon.   KENNETH F. RIPPLE, Circuit Judge

No. 89-1136	]	Appeal from the United States
	]	District Court for the
ANTHONY P. GOLUSZEK,	]	Northern District of Illinois
Plaintiff-Appellant,	]	Eastern Division
v.	]	No. 86 C 8412
H. P. SMITH,	]	Judge Ann Claire Williams
Defendant-Appellee.	]	

As of this date, there has been no response to this court's rule to show cause of October 18, 1990. Accordingly, pursuant to that rule and CR 31 (c) (2),

IT IS ORDERED that this appeal is DISMISSED for want of prosecution.

Anthony P. Goluszek
1239 Vincennes Ave.
Chicago Heights, Illinois 60411

Dear Mr. Goluszek:

The Chicago Police Department has received your mailgram dated August 12, 1992. Your correspondence was forwarded to me for initial investigation. After speaking to you by phone on October 20, 1992, I was able to determine that your compliant regards the conduct of several attorneys who participated in a federal court hearing before Judge Ann Williams.

In your conversation, you related your displeasure with the actions and comments of your attorney during your court appearance that involved allegations of sexual harassment and a workman's compensation claim.

Although this case was heard in Chicago, Illinois, there does not appear to be any criminal matter requiring the attention of the Chicago Police Department.

I am, however, providing you with the addressed and phone numbers of two other agencies that may be able to assist you in pressing for any civil or administrative remedies that you may seek. They are:

> Attorney Registration and Discipline Commission of the
> Supreme Court of Illinois
> 203 N. Wabash
> Chicago, Illinois
> 346-0690
>
> Legal Assistance Foundation
> 343 S. Dearborn
> Chicago, Illinois
> 341-1070

Sgt. Thomas Folliard
Bureau of Investigative Services
Chicago Police Department

January 23, 1984

Mr. Anthony P. Goluszek
1239 Vincennes Ave.
Chicago Heights, IL 60411

Dear Tony:

As you know, H.P. Smith has just completed another year of improved safety performance. Both the Chicago and Iowa City facilities achieved their respective 1983 safety objectives with seven and three OSHA recordable injuries. You, as an individual, played a significant role in the total team that provided this achievement by not experiencing a doctor treated case in 1983.

Our safety program included numerous policies, procedures, and practices designed to prevent injuries. These include such activities as monthly safety inspections, fire brigades, accident investigations, safe operating procedures, etc. More important, it includes the individual activities of all the employees. It has been through your efforts and safe work practices that H.P. Smith has been able to achieve our safety objectives for 1983.

I compliment you and thank you for your interest in our safety program which allowed you to have an injury-free year, and know we will receive your support in our safety program during 1984.

Sincerely,

H. P. Smith

J. L. Rooney
Vice President/General Manager

July 26, 1983

Mr. Anthony Goluszek
H. P. Smith Paper Co.

Dear Mr. Goluszek:

The grievance you submitted on June 30, 1983 was reviewed in a Second Step Meeting held on July 12, 1983.

The grievance review indicates that there has not been a violation of the Current Working Agreement, therefore, the grievance is denied.

Work assignments which you call "electrician work" will continue to be given to you just as they have been given to you and others in your job classification in the past. It is worth noting that you have successfully completed these assignments in the past, so your claim that you are not qualified in these areas is most difficult to understand. Employee in the Electronics Maintenance Man job classification have for a long period performed what you call "electrician work" such as bending conduit, pulling wires, installing switches or motors as well as periodically troubleshooting solid state circuitry.

This letter is a rewrite of the letter given you on July 13, 1983. The final paragraph was deleted pursuant to a grievance settlement.

Very truly yours,

H. P. SMITH PAPER CO.

John J. Mietlicki
Administrative Manager

10   J. L. Rooney
       J. R. Macfarlane
       C. Rodriguez
       M. P. Trendle

IN THE UNITED STATES DISTRICT COURT
NORTHERN DISTRICT OF ILLINOIS
EASTERN DIVISION

ANTHONLY GOLUSZEK,	)	
	)	
Plaintiff,	)	
	)	No. 86 C 8412
v.	)	
	)	Chicago, Illinois
H.P. SMITH, et al.	)	December 2, 1988
	)	2:00 p.m.
Defendants.	)	Trial

TRANSCRIPT OF PROCEEDINGS
BEFORE THE HONORABLE ANN C. WILLIAMS

APPEARANCES:

For Plaintiff:
MS. CLAUDIA ONEY
MR. MARK D. RIVERA
55 East Monroe Street
Suite 3420
Chicago, Illinois 60603

For the Defendants:
MAYER, BROWN & PLATT, by
MR. JAMES W. GLADDEN, JR.
MR. DAVID B. RITTER
190 South LaSalle Street
Chicago, Illinois 60603

Court Reporter:
Valarie M. Harris
Official Court Reporter
219 South Dearborn Street
Room 1928
Chicago, Illinois 60604
(312) 435-6891

1. A It was March 1978, I believe

2. Q And do you remember the position into which you were hired?

3. A I was hired as utility.

4. Q And how long did you stay in that position?

5. A It was a matter of a couple of months, and then I got a bid for an operator.

6. Q Okay. And how long did you stay in the operator's position?

7. A For the duration of my employment there.

8. Q And could you describe your duties as an operator?

9. A Well, would run their primary machines, which would cost paper.

10. Q Okay. Were you also a member of a union?

11. A Yes, Teamsters 714.

12. Q Other than the position of operator at H.P. Smith, did you have any other – were you actively engaged in any other position with H.P. Smith?

13. A I was a union steward.

14. Q And when were you the union steward?

15. A From about 1980 until about 1986. A little before 1986.

16. Q Could you tell us what a union steward does?

17. A Well, they would go to meetings with the company and work out differences, you know, problems between the union and the company, and they would also be there to protect employees.

18. Q And how many; of these meetings did you attend in all the

1. Q Do you recall what Tony Goluszek said during that meeting?
2. A Not really.
3. Q Do you recall what Bill Clemente said during that meeting?
4. A Bill stated that Ray was angry at Tony. And Ray was doing most of the talking, and Bill was kind of sitting there, and then Bill told Ray to calm down and, you know, let's get to the bottom of this and pretty much he said, well, if you can't be – you guys can't be fighting. Let's, you know, go back out there. We've got a job to do. Let's go out there and do it.
5. Q Do you recall at that meeting Bill Clemente saying that statement such as fucking in the ass about another person is just plain "shop talk"?
6. MR. GLADDEN: Your Honor, he's leading the witness.
7. THE COURT: Sustained.
8. MR. RIVERA: Your Honor, it's set out in the grievance form. It was signed by Tony Goluszek
9. THE COURT: Well, then refer him to the grievance form and have him read from that. You were leading.
10. MR. RIVERA: Okay, Judge.
11. BY MR. RIVERA:
12. Q Now, you signed this grievance form, is that correct?
13. A Right.

ANTHONY GOLUSZEK

1. Q   And when you signed the grievance form you – that was your signature attesting to what was stated in that grievance 3 form?

2. A   Well, pretty much. My signature is here for policy, because they won't accept a grievance unless it's signed by 6 the steward. So I didn't write this grievance, but I did sign it so the man was – he was feeling grieved. He wanted 8 to file a grievance, and in order to have a meeting I have to 9 sign this.

3. Q   What's said on the grievance form as to what Bill Clemente said, do you recall that being said?

4. A   Yes, because that was a big ting. Everybody picked on Tony.

5. MR. GLADDEN: Your Honor, I have to object.

6. THE COURT: Sustained. Disregard it. Strike it.

7. MR. RIVERA: Strike it as to everybody picking on Tony?

8. THE COURT: Yes. Yes.

9. Mr. RIVERA: But as to you ---

10. THE COURT: That portion can stand.

11. MR. RIVERA: Okay. Thank you, Judge.

12. BY MR. RIVERA:

13. Q   Now, after this meeting, did you have any other conversation with Tony Goluszek regarding this grievance form and that meeting?

1. I think that was there, but I just can't remember who was there.
2. BY MR. RIVERA:
3. Q   Okay. And can you tell us what was said?
4. A   Well, mainly we were asking him about girlfriends and 6 students, and it's kind – they were asking him if he had any sex with any girlfriends, and he was like saying no at the 8 time, and then they started getting to him about like homosexual relationships about, you know, screwing in the ass, student like that.
5. Q   Now, Mr. Luna, I want you to be, as best you can, to tell us exactly what was said. Now, was that the phrase that they used: Tony, have you ever had sex with a woman? What was the language that they used?
6. A   No, they would talk about Tony, did you ever fuck a girl. Did you ever, you know, did you ever fuck a girl in the ass and then like Corbett, said, well, did you ever fuck a guy in the ass, and he was like kind of like, you know, I don't talk like that. That's not my kind of thing.
7. Q   That's Tony's reaction?
8. A   That's Tony's reaction.
9. Q   Was there any other physical reaction to Tony?
10. A   Well, later on, like a few minutes later, Tony started working on the machine. He had to go check the hoist and he was up on the ladder and Al came by with a broom and then- stuck it in his butt and Tony like almost fell of the ladder in shock.
11. Q   Do you recall anything else that Tony Goluszek did in response to that?
12. A   Well, he told me at that time that's he not like that and that, you know, people were actually bothering him.
13. Were you ever one of them?
14. A   At first, yes. I was like one of them. We just goofed around with him and have fun, but then he told me it bothers him.
15. Q   And what did you do then?

16. A So I stopped and I didn't, you know, didn't harass him or nothing like that. I tried not to, you know. And if I did, I told him, Tony, I'm sorry. I don't mean it like that, you know, if he thought I was wrong, you know.

17. Q Now, after Al Corbett stuck him with a stick, did you see what Al Corbett did after that or said?

18. A No. That's all I can remember, comes real clear with him standing on the ladder and him going like this with the broom.

19. Q Any other occasion where you witnessed this?

20. A Well, anytime we got by the machine and we called for maintenance and we need an electrician, Tony would come over and usually we'd get a couple of guys and get around and start talking about this stuff.

1. Q We had a chance to review today a copy of your personnel file that was provided to me by H.P. Smith. Is that the address and telephone number that appear on your employee personnel data change that was in this file?

2. A Which document?

3. Q It's the employee personnel data change. Your telephone and address appear in that file?

4. A Yes, it is signed by me. That was the document that was signed by me when H.P. was sold to James Rivers.

5. Q Thank you. Would you please give the Court a brief description of your employment background and educational background?

6. A Educationally I graduated from Loyola in 1969 with a bachelor's of arts, and graduated in 1976 from Loyola with master's in business administration in personnel industrial relations. Been in the human resources area a little over 19 years. 10 years of which I worked for H.P. Smith, then Phillips Products, which were then subsidiaries of Phillips Petroleum. I worked for several other companies in varying capacities.

7. Q After you left H.P. Smith where did you go to work?

8. A I worked for a period of about five months with Keith Ross & Associates.

9. Q And after that?

10. A I worked a year at the Illinois Local Labor Relations.

1. MS. ONEY: Your Honor, I have one witness who's been waiting since about 2 or 3. I don't think he'll take long. We have – I've received a stipulation from counsel 4 as to an exhibit that will substantially cut down the --
2. THE COURT: All right. Bring him in.
3. 6 MS. ONEY: I've got a baby-sitting problem, so if you want to stop, but I think we can do this quickly.
4. 8THE COURT: Well, bring him in. We'll see.
5. I'll recess if we can't.
6. MS. ONEY: Okay.
7. (Witness sworn.)
8. JOHN MIETLICKI, PLAINTIFF'S WITNESS, FIRST DULY SWORN DIRECT EXAMINATION
9. BY MS. ONEY:
10. Q   Please state your name for the record.
11. A   John Mietlicki.
12. Q   Where do you reside?
13. A   3510 West 66th Street, Chicago.
14. THE COURT: Would you spell your last name?
15. THE WITNESS: M-i-e-t-l-i-c-k-i.
16. BY MS. ONEY:
17. Q   How long have you lived at that address?
18. A   Approximately 14 years.
19. Q   What is your telephone number?
20. A   776-8088.

1. Board
2. Q And after that?
3. A And subsequent to that I worked two years, nine months Blue Cross/Blue Shield of Illinois.
4. Q All right. Thank you. When did you leave your employment at H.P. Smith?
5. A April of 1984
6. Q All right.
7. MS. ONEY: May I approach the witness?
8. THE COURT: Yes.
9. BY MS. ONEY:
10. Q I'm showing you a document marked Plaintiff's Exhibit
11. No. 72.
12. MS. ONEY: Your Honor doesn't have a copy of this but I'm going to tender this to you as soon as the witness identifies it. This has been stipulated to.
13. BY MS. ONEY:
14. Q Do you recognize that document?
15. THE COURT: All right. It will be admitted.
16. (Plaintiff's Exhibit No. 72 was received in evidence.)
17. THE WITNESS: I have not previously seen the document. It wasn't addressed to me. I didn't get a copy.
18. BY MS. ONEY:
19. Q But you read it today. Is that right?
20. A Yes, I have.

1. Q And do you have – are the facts as they are set out in that document approximately correct?
2. A I believe as a transcript of the interview that took place on April 6th, they are correct. They're essentially 5 correct.
3. Q And the items set out in that document, do they – what do they represent?
4. A They represent an interview between James Rooney and myself on April 6th.
5. Q And just very briefly, the subject matter of that interview?
6. A Issues, issues involving alleged sexual harassment that – feeling was that there was a discussion on my part things that I did that constituted alleged sexual harassment.
7. Q And what was the result of that interview?
8. A I resigned.
9. MS. ONEY: Your Honor, this is the Court's copy of this.
10. BY MS. ONEY:
11. Q Did you believe yourself to have engaged in sexual harassment?
12. A No, I did not.
13. Q All right. Where you familiar with an employee while you were at H.P. Smith named Tony Goluszek?

1. A   Yes.
2. Q   Would you please describe your contact you remember with Tony Goluszek?
3. A   Tony was an electronics maintenance man. I had mostly had dealings with him in grievance issues. There were other times when I would walk through the plant and he and I would talk.
4. Q   Do you remember Tony making complaints when you were employed at H.P. Smith?
5. A   Tony, Tony complained about a lot of things during the period of time I was there.
6. Q   What do you remember him complaining about?
7. A   Well, he complained of – on several occasions of while he was performing work on a ladder some of the forklift drivers coming too close and attempting to hit him and knock him off. He indicated he was afraid of that. He complained of a procedure that required him to go up on a high-bay warehouse and work on the crane that was about 60 feet in the air. He felt the procedure to do the work up there was unsafe. And he complained of a lot of different things. He said that he was being harassed by the guys in the maintenance department, the people on the floor.
8. Q   Did he specify the kind of harassment?
9. A   Initially no. He claimed that the people on the floor used to kid him, and it was a lot of different people. He never really mentioned any – any names specifically, but they would kid him about a lot of things.
10. Q   And when did he first report this kidding to you?
11. A   I couldn't precisely say, but I know it was subsequent to the time that James Rivers acquired H.P. Smith.
12. A   I believe it was October-mid-October of '83.
13. Q   And what action did you take when he reported this kidding to you?
14. A   Well, he complained about a number of things specifically on the harassment. I did not investigate it, per se, but advised Jim

MacFarlane who was the maintenance superintendent that Tony
was complaining again about a number of things and maybe --

15. Q   Did you have a meeting with Mr. MacFarlane?

16. A   I think I – I don't know that it was a formal --it was a discussion.
I stopped him and said Tony was.

17. Q   When did that occur?

18. A   It was shortly after Tony – Tony had mentioned to me about --

19. Q   At the end of '83?

20. A   Possibly.

21. Q   And what was said?

22. A   Pardon me?

23. Q   What was said? What did Jim MacFarlane say to you

I hereby certify that the above entitled matter is true and correct.

_______________________________   _______________________________

      Reporter   Date

_______________________________   _______________________________

   Official Reporter   Date

1. A Yes.
2. Q What's the policy, if you would please summarize it, regarding making complaints directly to the company?
3. A Basically it's --
4. THE COURT: Excuse me. Counsel, it's in the document. I have the document. There's no need for him to read the document.
5. 8 BY MS. ONEY:
6. Q All right. Did you consider this particular policy in your capacity as industrial relations manager as something that would supplement the union grievance procedure?
7. A It was an open-door communications policy, and any employee was not prevented from utilizing this procedure without talking to your supervisor about a problem, and they could certainly do that apart from actually filing a formal grievance and it was commonly done that way.
8. Q Did you consider the – you were familiar with the union contract?
9. A Yes.
10. Q Is that correct?
11. A Yes.
12. Q Did you consider it to cover an employee who had a problem with sexual harassment?
13. A It could. Actually the contract covered any legitimate – any problem that an employee wished to grieve supporting and implementing this policy."
14. Q Do you think that policy applied to Tony Goluszek while you were the industrial relations manager?
15. A It was a policy that applied to everybody at the company.
16. Q Was it followed regarding Tony Goluszek?
17. A If Tony Goluszek was an employee –
18. Q Pardon me?
19. A If Tony Goluszek was an employee it would have applied to him the same way as any other employee.

20. 11MS. ONEY: May I approach the witness?

21. 12THE COURT: Yes.

22. 13MS. ONEY: No. 70. This has already been admitted.

23. BY MS. ONEY:

24. Q   Would you identify that for the record, please?

25. A   It's the employee communications procedure that was put out under John VanBuskirk's signature who was then president of H.P. Smith.

26. Q   Did you assist in preparing that?

27. A   I was involved. Really I didn't write it. Again this was – a lot that came out of Phillips Corp. that went into this. This was pretty much a procedure that was implemented company wide.

28. Q Your name is mentioned, isn't it?

29. Q The portion concerning harassment, did you write that portion?

30. A   This was basically the policy that had been issued through Phillips Petroleum Company, that we were all the personnel managers and industrial relations managers were advised – were enforced at subsidiary units. You want me to read it or –

31. Q   Any way you want to describe the policy.

32. A   Well, I'll just read it. It's easier. Phillips Petroleum Company is committed to maintaining a work environment with respect to privacy and dignity of the individual. Physical or verbal harassment of employees or applicants for employment is incompatible with that principle and with acceptable job performance. Harassment includes any conduct that has the purpose of or effect of unreasonably interfering with an individual's work performance or creating an intimidating, hostile and offensive working environment. Inappropriate jokes, slurs tricks, name calling, sexual advancements or comments can constitute harassment.

33. The company's internal communications procedure provides for all employees the avenue through which problems such as harassment can be reported and addressed without fear of reprisal. All employees of Phillips Petroleum Company and subsidiary companies are accountable for manager at H.P. Smith did you ever have occasion to deal with any charges of discrimination?

   ANTHONY GOLUSZEK

34. A   Yes, we did have charges filed, handicap discrimination charges and others.

35. Q   Did you have a policy, or were you aware of EEO rules and regulations regarding retaining documents?

36. A   Other than the fact that if a charge was filed we amass all the documents relative to the specific charge or medical 9 records, whatever the case might be, and retain them in the is crimination charge file.

37. THE COURT: Is that about it, counsel?

38. MS. ONEY: Very very close, yes.

39. THE COURT: How long do you think your cross will be? I just want to know if you'll be able to do it in a few minutes or whether we'll have the witness back.

40. MR. GLADDEN: My guess is I can get done in five minutes.

41. MS. ONEY: Your Honor, may I approach the witness?

42. THE COURT: You may.

43. BY MS. ONEY:

44. Q   Exhibit No. 68, would you please identify this for the record?

45. A   This was a notice that was posted at H.P. Smith under my signature regarding access to employee exposure of medical records and harassment, general comments such as that.

46. Q   How many complaints did you hear from Tony directly 3 during the year 1984 concerning sex talk on the factory floor?

47. A   I guess apart from the, you know, my awareness into 6 this grievance, there might have been one other occasion when he mentioned it.

48. Q   Did you ever take any action about this alleged sexual harassment during the year 1984?

49. A   I was only there for under four months. I did not take any – that was basically what I passed out to the main superintendent.

50. Q   Did you ever have a meeting with J.T. Webb concerning this alleged sexual harassment by Tony?

51. A   I don't know that I had a meeting. I guess I had a discussion. I mentioned it to him that Tony had been by complaining about this, and he indicated, yeah, he was aware, because Tony had stopped him.

52. Q And did you and he make any effort to resolve this problem or was there --

53. A I didn't question it. It was just a mention. It was just a mention in passing that Tony had been by and mentioned it to me and the issue of the grievance. That was it. It wasn't any kind of a formal discussion

54. Q While you were in your position as industrial relations specifically recall.

55. Q Do you remember any discussions involving Tony's claim of sexual harassment subsequent to returning that grievance to him?

56. A With Tony?

57. Q Tes.

58. A And Carlos?

59. Q With Mr. Luna or Mr. Rodriguez.

60. A With Mr. Luna or Mr. Rodriguez.

61. Q That's correct.

62. A I really can't recall. I might have mentioned something to them, because they were really the responsible stewards on the shift. And I said, you know, I'm returning the grievance. It might have been kind of like that. I can't specifically – it wasn't a formalized meeting.

63. Q Now, you received complaints from Tony Goluszek during the year 1984 when you would encounter him on a one to one basis. Is that correct?

64. A Every once in a while if he'd see me and when I'd be walking through the plant he, you know, he'd make comments to me that they're at it again or they're doing – I couldn't really categorize them in any particular way, but typically he would stop me at times, and tell me about problems he was having or there were – I know he said that they were picking on him again for not doing his job or vice president of manufacturing who was involved again with 2 myself and all the parties. So it was, you know, really the 3 next step in the process except it involved that manufacturing head.

65. Q Step 3 decision maker in 1984 would be whom?

66. A   In 1984 it would have been at that point J. Webb, because he was vice president of manufacturing.

67. 8 MS. ONEY: At that time, Your Honor, may I 9 approach the witness?

68. THE COURT: Yes.

69. BY MS. ONEY:

70. Q Do you remember this grievance, Mr. Mietlicki?

71. THE COURT: Which is which document?

72. MS. ONEY: I'm sorry. No. 4, Judge.

73. THE WITNESS: Yes, I recall the grievance.

74. BY MS. ONEY:

75. Q Did you conduct any investigation into that document?

76. A   No, I don't believe that there was any investigation at all conducted into it, because of the fact that the grievance was not filed on a timely basis and was returned to the grievant.

77. Q   Did you have a meeting subsequent to returning that document to the grievant with the union stewards, Tony Luna and Carlos Rodriguez?

78. A   I might have had a discussion with them. I can't someone had disciplinary action specifically, or really could be any other action by supervision, management, if, in fact, something was done, and the employee felt he had a 4 legitimate grievance, a grievance was filed and first heard 5 with the supervisor and the superintendent.

79. Q   That's step one.

80. A   That's step one, right. And if, in fact, a grievance was denied at that point then it was brought to me, and said that we want to proceed to the next step. That's when I got involved, and typically a meeting was scheduled with the supervisor, superintendent and myself, the grieving party, the steward, and we had a meeting to sit down and basically rehash the issue again.

81. Q   And who would make the decision after this rehash?

82. A   I would make the decision. Of course, it would be made after discussion again with the superintendent, the supervisor, if, in fact, it happened at times in Step 2 of the grievance that we felt the action that was taken was inappropriate; it might have been reduced or eliminated.

83. Q   But you signed the letters?

84. A Yes, I did. I issued that step of the grievance, and if the grieving party did not agree with that decision we went on to the next step.

85. Q At the Step 3 level, who would make the decision?

86. A That was---well, it was generally the plant manager, and---

87. A He said he'd check into it.

88. Q Now, you were personnel manager at that point, right, isn't that basically --

89. A I was industrial relations manager. They're basically the same thing.

90. Q They are basically the same thing.

91.   Did you ever see any warning letters written or any 9 action at all taken by Jim MacFarlane?

92. A Relative to what?

93. Q On the issue of Tony's complaints.

94. A I don't recall that I've ever seen any documentation like that.

95. Q Would letters like that he copied to you as personnel manager, or would it be sent to the personnel department?

96. A If, in fact, it was formal disciplinary action we made it a policy that formal disciplinary action should be sent to us for insertion into the employee's file, yes, if it was formal disciplinary action.

97. Q Do you know whether or not MacFarlane did anything?

98. A I have no knowledge whether he did anything.

99. Q Would you please describe the personnel policies at H.P. Smith regarding union grievances? What's the — at what part of that process did you become involved?

100.   A I would become involved in Step 2 of the grievance.

Anthony T. Goluszek
3034 Chgo. Rd, Apt.7
S.C.H., IL, 60411

Supreme Court
1 First St. N.E.
Washington, D.C. U.S.A.

Dear Sirs:

As far as I am concern I won in the 7th Circuit because they did not respond to my complaint about Fed. Judges with 7th circuits and these diaries of the 7th Circuit. I could go to your court, just tell me time and date to appear.

Sincerely,

3034 Chgo Rd Apt. 7
So. Chgo. Hts
Il. 60411

Mr. Higgins
Supreme Court
1 First St. N.E.
Washington D.C., USA

Dear Sirs:

If the 7th Circuit letter was not done right, they would not put seal on it. Must be acceptable at Supreme Court and 7th to harass; rape and fraud.

Sincerely,

Anthony Goluszek
(708) 833-5049

Anthony Goluszek
24473
8/17/07

Mr. Goluszek is seen today in a fifteen minute medication check. He says he has been out of the Tegretol now for quite a while. I confronted him again that not only do I think he needs the Tegretol for his emotions and moods but I also think he needs it for the seizure that he had. He says he felt the medicine was just too much on his liver even though no one told him in any kind of blood test that he was having any issues with his liver. He also wants to cut the Paxil to 10 mg per day because he feels the 20 mg per day is too strong also. He denies any intention of harming himself or anyone else. He denies any hallucinations. He denies any paranoia.

He has become much more compulsive with the obsession about his prior sexual harassment lawsuit that ended his working career. He still obsessively is trying to send the paperwork to different places even different states trying to get someone to take the case to refile all of the motions. He seems to take in stride though when people tell him there is really nothing they can do because of how long ago this all transpired. His sister is now living with him so at least someone is there keeping an eye on him just in case he were to have a seizure. He is not driving. He has not had anything that even resembles a seizure he says. Affect is bright. He is interacting with friend and going out on a daily basis. Even the jerking movements in his muscles that he has always had since i met him, seem to doing a little bit better. Sleep and appetite are fine. He says he is very consistently eating a better diet.

Assessment
Chronic Schizophrenia
Obsessive Compulsive Disorder

Treatment Plan:
I did agree he could decrease Paxil to 10 mg and he agreed he would go back to the Tegretol 200 mg q am and 400 mg nightly to make sure he had no chance of having a seizure. He will return in two months for medication

monitoring. He will call in the interim if any problems arise and agreed
with the recommendation for today.

40

____

Mary E. Belford MD
MEB:kjm

1. THE COURT: All right. You may take the stand

2. MR. RIVERA: We'd like to call Tony – Anthony Luna.

3. (Witness sworn.)

4. ANTONIO LUNA, PLAINTIFF'S WITNESS, DULY SWORN

5. DIRECT EXAMINATION

6. BY MR. RIVERA:

7. Q   Could you state your name for the record, please?

8. A   Antonio Luna, Jr.

9. THE COURT REPORTER: Could you spell your name, please?

10. THE WITNESS: L-u-n-a.

11. BY MR. RIVERA:

12. Q   Mr. Luna, where do you live?

13. A   I live at 10330 South 82nd Avenue in Palos Hills.

14. Q   And how old are you?

15. A   I'm 29.

16. Q   And how is it that you come to appear before this Court today?

17. A   I was subpoenaed for the plaintiff.

18. Q   Mr. Luna, could you just give us a brief outline of your educational background starting with high school and going to any post high school education?

19. A   Okay. I graduated from Oak Lawn Community High School in January 1977, and I attended Moraine Valley Community College for about a year. And then I was off – I quit school for Luna – direct about ten years, nine years, and I went back to DeVry, and I got a diploma.

20. Q   And while you were at high school, was there any specific area of concentration in which you concentrated?

21. A   Automotive technology.

22. Q   And when you went to one year in college right after high school, was there a specific area of study that you concen-8 trated it?

23. A   Automotive technology.

24. Q   Now, after you left college after the one year, what did you do?

25. A   I went to work for H.P. Smith.

26. Q   And how long did you work for H.P. smith?

27. A   It was about eight years, I think, close to nine.

28. Q   And then what did you do after you left H.P. Smith?

29. A   I started with Illinois Bell.

30. Q   And you said you went to college at what time? You went back to college between what?

31. A   In 1984, July 1984 I went back to college.

32. Q   Until?

33. A   Until 1986.

34. Q   And did you state the colleges you went to?

35. A   Moraine Valley College.

36. Q   No, the second college.

37. A   No. I just went to Moraine Valley. Then I went to DeVry.

1. Q   And what did you study at DeVry?
2. A   Electronic technology.
3. Q   Are you now employed?
4. A   Yes, I am.
5. Q   In what?
6. A   Illinois Bell.
7. Q   What do you do there?
8. A   I'm a central offi ce technician. I run their switch.
9. Q   Okay. Do you recall the date that you were hired for H.P. Smith?
10. A   It was March 1978, I believe.
11. Q   And do you remember the position into which you were hired?
12. A   I was hired as utility.
13. Q   And how long did you stay in that position?
14. A   It was a matter of a couple of months, and then I got a bid for an
        operator.
15. Q   Okay. And how long did you stay in the operator's position?
16. A   For the duration of my employment there.
17. Q   And could you describe your duties as an operator?
18. A   Well, would run their primary machines, which would coat paper.
19. Q   Okay. Were you also a member of a union?
20. A   Yes, Teamsters 714.
21. Q   Other than the position of operator at H.P. Smith, did you have
        any other – were you actively engaged in any other position with
        H.P. Smith?
22. A   I was a union steward.
23. Q   And when were you the union steward?
24. A   From about 1980 until about 1986. A little before 1986.
25. Q   Could you tell us what a union steward does?
26. A   Well, they would go to meetings with the company and work
        out differences, you know, problems between the union and the
        company, and they would also be there to protect employees.
27. Q   And how many of these meetings did you attend in all the years
        that you were a steward?

28. A   I'd say hundreds of them.

29. Q   How many grievances did you pursue while you were a union steward?

30. A   Probably hundreds. It might not be that many, but it was quite a bit.

31. Q   Now, generally could you describe what these grievance meetings involved?

32. A   Most of them were for attendance problems.

33. Q   And who would be at these meetings?

34. A   Well, usually the immediate supervisor, the foreman, the person who was being accused of whatever, and then the union steward.

1. Q   And generally when you attended these meetings did you 2 notice any kind of note taking by any of the – by any 3 individual during those meetings?

2. A   No, not really. On occasion, like the steward – I took some notes, but I don't have any of my notes.

3. 6MR. RIVERA: your Honor, may I approach the witness?

4. Q   Mr. Luna, I'd like to show you what has been marked Plaintiff's Exhibit No. 3, which by stipulation is offered into evidence.

5. THE COURT: Admitted.

6. (Plaintiff's Exhibit No. 3 was received in evidence.)

7. Q   Do you recognize that document?

8. A   Well, not really, but I've seen the documents like this, not this particular one.

9. Q   Okay. This document refers to – well, why don't I let you keep that. This document refers to Mr. Goluszek having an injury for a year in 1983. Do you recall having a conversation with Tony Goluszek regarding this letter?

10. A   No, I don't.

11. Q   The letter also refers to a safety program, and in the second paragraph it starts out: "Our safety program". Were you aware of any safety program that was at H.P. Smith?

12. A   Yes.

13. Q   Could you describe that program for us?

1 Q   January of what year?

2 A   '84.

3 Q   And do you remember --

4 A   That's the one with Ray Goytia, I think.

5 Q   And do you remember who was present during this?

6 A   That was Leo, Bill Clemente, Ray Goytia.

Q   Well, I'm talking about the time that you're talking about with what Leo said. Who was present during that 9 conversation?

A   Leo, Bill, me and Tony.

Q   What did Mr. Karpinski say to you?

A   When we were talking out of the office he said that he was getting to stick a six-shooter up Tony's ass to get him to work faster.

Q   Did Tony Goluszek make any response?

A   He didn't, I don't think. He told me later to see what he said, but not right away he didn't say nothing. When we walked away he didn't say anything about it.

Q   Did he say anything to you later?

A   Yes, he said did you hear what he said? I said, yeah, I heard him.

Q   Do you know how much later that was when you had that conversation?

A   It was about five or ten minutes later, right when we walked away.

 Anthony Goluszek

1. A. We're going to file it a little late.
2. Q But you have no recollection of that conversation either, do you?
3. A No.
4. Q Okay. So you don't know whether a grievance was filed
5. 6 on this or not, isn't that right?
6. A Right.
7. Q Now, if an employee doesn't file a grievance, then it's appropriate for the company to treat this as a written warning in his file, isn't that right?
8. A Yes, I would imagine.
9. Q Okay. And they can take future discipline based upon this letter having been placed in the file and no grievance filed with it, isn't that right?
10. A Yes, sir.
11. Q Pardon?
12. A Yes, sir.
13. Q Okay.
14. A That's what the company is all about.
15. Q Now, let me direct your attention to Exhibit 4.
16. A I have it.
17. Q Okay. Now, this particular grievance says: "Date of grievance, 1-27-84, is that correct?
18. A Right.
19. Q Now, this would indicate that the grievance, the event which created the grievance occurred on that date, isn't that right?
20. A Right
21. Q And what occurred on that date was the meeting with Ray Goytia, Tony Goluszek, you and Mr. Clements and you say Mr. 6 Karpinski was there.
22. A Right.
23. Q And this is the meeting where Mr. Karpinski made a comment when he came away from the meeting about a six-shooter?
24. A Right.

25. Q And at that meeting Mr. Goytia was very mad, wasn't he?

26. A Yes.

27. Q He felt that he was being picked on?

28. A Right.

29. Q And as I understand your recollection was Mr. Clemente said, cool down, calm down, we've got to work together.

30. Let's go out and work and get it done, get the job done, correct?

31. A Right.

32. Q Now, this written grievance is dated 2-7-84, is that right?

33. A Right.

34. Q That means this written grievance as of 2-7-84, that's Step 2, correct?

35. A Right.

36. Q So the first step was 1-26-84; the second step is 2-7-84, correct?

37. A Right.

38. Q You have to say yes or no.

39. A I said right. Yes.

40. Q Now, look at Exhibit No. 5. This is the letter denying the grievance which is Exhibit No. 4, correct?

41. A Yes, it is.

42. Q And it says: "This grievance you first submitted for Step 2 consideration on February 7th, 1984, and your own statement, Step 1 was denied on January 26th." And so, it's denied as untimely, correct?

43. A Right.

44. Q Now, you had a right, did you not, as the union, and Mr. Goluszek had the right, if you thought the time limit was unfairly being called, to take this to the next step, didn't you?

45. A Yes.

46. Q You didn't, isn't that right?

47. A Well, we talked to Mr. Mietlicki after that.

48. Q My question, Mr. Luna, you didn't take this grievance to Step 3?

49. No, I didn't.

50. Q And when he turned it down for being untimely you did not pursue that to a higher level, is that correct?

    Anthony Goluszek

51. A   Right. But you've got to understand, I mean you can't pursue that much because the union wouldn't back you up. So there was a lot of things that we never took to the third step because, I mean, after a while it's just meaningless.

52. Q   Your testimony was no grievance – time limits were never called on grievances. That's your testimony, as I understand it. But you're saying when this was turned down 9 for having a time limit called on it you didn't pursue it because the union wouldn't support you, is that your testimony?

53. A   Yes.

54. Q   Now, why wouldn't the union support you?

55. A   Because they'[re not going to come down for petty stuff like this. I mean the company writes letters all the time and you've got a thousand files of letters

56. Q   My understanding of your testimony, Mr. Luna, is that this grievance, which was filed on the 7th and turned down on the 8th, that's the first time or the only time, I think you said, the only time that you saw a grievance turned down that quickly, is that right?

57. A   Right.

58. Q   Okay. Let me show you – and by that quickly, you mean turned down the next day?

59. A   Right. They gave us a letter dated the next day.

60. THE COURT: Oh, okay.

61. MR. GLADDEN: I hope.

62. BY MR. GLADDEN:

63. Q   Mr. Luna, going back to – looking at 4 and 5 again.

64. When the company turned the grievance down as being untimely, did Mr. Goluszek complain to you about that?

65. A   I don't recall.

66. Q   Did he accuse you of being negligent?

67. A   I don't think so, not that I recall.

68. Q   To your knowledge, did he file an unfair labor charge saying you had been negligent in not pursuing his grievance?

69. A   Not that I know of.

70. Q   But he never complained to you, as far as you can recall?

71. A   Right.

72. Q   Mr. Luna, did Mr. Goluszek ever bring Playboy magazines himself
       to the plant?

73. A   Not that I can remember.

74. Q   Did he have them at the house when you shared a house with him?

75. A   Not that I know of.

76. Q   You don't recall?

77. A   Not that I know of.

78. Q   Not that you know of. Your conversation with Mr. Clemente,
       when you asked for a written apology, that occurred in his office;
       that was between you and him?

79. A   Right.

80. Q   And he said no, I'm not going to put it in writing; I stand beside
       what I said?

81. A   Yes.

82. Q   Did he, in fact, orally apologize to Mr. Goluszek for saying it was
       "shop talk"?

83. A   Yes.

84. Q   So before the grievance was even filed, Mr. Clemente had orally
       apologized; he simply was not going to put the apology 11 in
       writing?

85. A   Right.

86. MR. GLADDEN: I have no further questions.

87. MR. RIVERA: We have no redirect.

88. THE COURT: All right. You're excused.

(END OF EXCERPT)

<u>EXHIBIT # B</u>

ANSWER TO INTERROGATORY NOs.

2,3,4,5,6,8

December 1976

Operators at No. 2, 3, 4, 7, 14 Slitter machines on night shift constant questions and statements to Plaintiff as to why he is not married, why he had no girlfriend, and that you have to be married to work here, etc. No oral or written report was made.

Winter 1977

Same operators to Plaintiff "If you can't fix the machine, we'll have to call your daddy in" referring to Foreman Mike Byczek, national origin – Polish. Plaintiff reported to night supervisor Cal Adair. His response was to later say the same things to Plaintiff in Spring 1978.

Winter 1978

Night Supervisor, Cal Adair telling Plaintiff that "if you can't fix the machine, it will be the sausage factor for you," and that what Plaintiff needs is to "get married and get some of that soft pink smelly stuff that's between the legs of a woman." Plaintiff responded by asking Mr. Adair not to comment about Plaintiff's personal life.\

Spring 1979

Operators at No. 3 and 7 Slitter machines on night shift. Statements to Plaintiff that he should be married and that he should go out with Kathy Kristein, employee of Defendant– jeep driver. That "she would take good care" of him. That "she fucks." Plaintiff reported this conduct to Cal Adair. Mr. Adair's response was to later say to Plaintiff that "if we can't get Tony to fix the machine fast enough, we'll have to call in Kathy Kristein to fix Tony.

Winter 1981

After Plaintiff returned to night shift, Alan Corbert said to Plaintiff "So you didn't get along with your daddy on days? (reference to Mike Byczek) Did you get any pussy anytime?" Soon thereafter Al Corbert and Willie Smith, both machine operators would continuously ask the Plaintiff, "Hey Tony, did you get any pussy today?" After asking Corbert and Smith to not comment about his personal affairs, Plaintiff reported this harassment to Bill Clemente. Clemente told Plaintiff he would talk to Corbert and Smith.

Spring 1982

Corbert again comments: "Hey Tony did you get fucked yet. You better do something before your cock falls off" Plaintiff told Corbert to "go to hell." Corbert on another occasion comments: "Hey Tony did you get any black pussy lately. You know when you get some black pussy you don't come back. Corbert on another occasion calls Plaintiff over to him to show him a nude woman in a Playboy Magazine, and says: "Hey Tony come over here and check this out. Wouldn't you fuck her?" Plaintiff responded that he would. Plaintiff reported incidents to Bill Clemente and he said he would check it out.

Summer 1982

Corbert again says: "Hey Tony, you going to get any pussy this summer." Then Willie Smith says: "If you can Tony, try to get some black pussy this summer. It's black on the outside, but pink on the inside and just as good. Boy, you won't regret it. I guarantee it." Pliantiff responded by thanking Smith for the advice. Corbert, Smith and operators on No. 2, 3, 4, 6, and 7 slitter machines constant comments: "Hey Tondy look at this pussy. Wouldn't you like to fuck it in this position?" (Nude woman in the Playboy magazine). "I bet there's women in H.P. Smith that are just as good? "Tony, when are you going to get fucked. Staying a virgin all your life is no fun. We're going to have to get you fucked. How about Kathy (jeep driver for Defendant)? No, Terry (Machine operator for Defendant)? No, Edna (jeep driver for Defendant)? She gives good blow jobs. You like blow jobs don't you Tony? I know you do. I got it. Wanda Jackson (machine operator for Defendant) on days. Perfect tits and fantastic ass.

 ANTHONY GOLUSZEK

Boy, she would give you your money's worth. Hey, Tony how would you like sticking your nose up her.?" "Hey Tony, fuck that work and come over here and read these electrical drawings (actually they were Playboy Magazines). This will tell you how to fix it." Plaintiff responded that such conduct was a distraction, a waste of time, and adversely affecting his job performance. Plaintiff constantly asked that such conduct stop. Plaintiff reported to Bill Clemente of such conduct and that Playboy magazines were being seen all over the plant. Clemente said he would do something.

Fall 1982

Al Corbert, stated to Plaintiff while standing with Willie Smith, Yevon Jerome (mechanic) and Fernando Ferandez (jeep operator): "Hey Tony, wouldn't you like to get your small cock in this shit (showing Plaintiff a picture of a nude woman from a Playboy Magazine?" Smith then said: "Boy, I know Tony would jump right in. Look at him change colors on his face. He loves that shit." Then, Ferandez responds: "His (Plaintiff) cock couldn't handle it. He'd have to try it on me first. Jerome then states: "Tony never got into any body. Oh, you're not a man until you put your cock in your first ass and enjoy the shit and its smell." Plaintiff reported to Foreman Howie Strowshine of this incident. Plaintiff was told that since Cal Adair is Corbert's uncle nothing will happen on this, and that Plaintiff should forget about this. Plaintiff then made a report to Bill Clemente. Clemente told Plaintiff to forget about it, and that if he persisted with these complaints, he would be fired.

Spring 1983

Al Corbert stated to Plaintiff: "Hey Tony did you get any ass yet. You know those black girls got nice big boodies. Plaintiff again reported to Bill Clemente, insisted that something be done. Clemente responded that Plaintiff would have to put up with it a little longer so that Clemente could personally observe such conduct and fire those responsible.

May 27, 1983

Yvone Jerome asked Plaintiff, if he had ever had put his "dick in a women's ass" and would Plaintiff allow some men to do the same to him. Plaintiff responded that "You know a lot of people would kill a person for saying that." Jerome then said that he was a Vietnam Vet, and could kill Plaintiff with a piano wire. Plaintiff responded: "Well, why don't you take a swing, and see how far you can go. I bet when I deck you you'll fall to pieces.

Summer 1983

Fernando Ferandez stated to Plaintiff that he wanted to go "bisexual" with Plaintiff. Plaintiff responded that "the only way you will go with one is with your teeth knocked out." Ferandez responded that he enjoyed SM. Plaintiff responded: "You're helpless. Yevone Jerome asked Plaintiff if he had ever raped a woman or a little girl. Plaintiff responded "No have you?" Plaintiff reported these incidents to Bill Clemente. He stated that he would handle it.

Fall 1983

Yvone Jerome accused Plaintiff and Tony Luna of being gay, because at one time, Plaintiff and Luna had shared an apartment. Plaintiff told Jerome to "get out of here before I puty you way. Plaintiff reported this to Bill Clemente and Tony Luna. Luna told Plaintiff that there was little he could do, that others were complaining of the same thing, but that nothing is being done about it.

Winter 1983

Al Corbert came up behind Plaintiff with a stick and stuck it up Plaintiff's back side while yelling boodie, boodie man, and then ran off. Plaintiff reported this to Bill Clemente stating that he can not take this harassment much longer. Clemente stated that "don't worry, you won't be here much longer." Plaintiff reported to Luna and Luna told him that he was aware of the problem, that others were also complaining, and that he would pursue the matter.

January 1984

Yevone Jerome told Plaintiff he was going to "hypnotize" him to be a "boodie man. Al Corbert again came up from behind Plaintiff repeating his earlier conduct with a stick while yelling boodie, boodie, boodie man, and then ran off.

August 29, 1983

Tony Luna (union steward) stated to Plaintiff" "How come my dog is pregnant; did you knock her up?" Plaintiff responded: "Tony, how would you like it if I said that to you about your old lady?" Luna responded that he would beat Plaintiff up. Plaintiff responded that that was the way he felt about what Luna said.

January 26, 1984

At a meeting with Bill Clemente, Roy Goytia, Tony Luna, and Plaintiff among others Goytia complained to Clemente that Plaintiff was harassing him. Plaintiff told Clemente of all the harassment he has continually faced. Clemente responded that "Well Tony, in your case fucking ass about another person is just plain shop talk." Plaintiff and Luna disagreed. After the meeting, Plaintiff and Luna decided that if nothing was done in a few days, they would file a grievance.

February 1984

Plaintiff asked for a meeting with Jim Rooney, Vice-President, regarding the sexual harassment. No meeting ever occurred Plaintiff's grievance was denied review due to missing a time limitation. Plaintiff appealed decision, but nothing further was heard.

Leo Karpinski, while in the Slitter Office with Plaintiff and Wanda Johnson, asked Plaintiff how he would like to have a date with Ms. Johnson. Karpinski then asked Mrs. Johnson if she would go out with Plaintiff. Ms. Johnson left the office. Another time, Karpenski told Plaintiff that he should get a "six-shooter up your ass."

March 1984

Yevone Jerome told Plaintiff what "I hear you turned your boss in for talking about ass sex. You know you like it." Plaintiff asked to be left alone.

Willie Smithy told Plaintiff that he should not have complained about this "ass sex" since "a little shit on your dick never hurt any body." Bill Clemente called Plaintiff over to No. 14 machine and asked why it wasn't fixed faster, and that the problem with the machine is Plaintiff's breathing. Plaintiff suggested that maybe Clemente could remedy his breathing by stepping outside with Plaintiff.

April 1, 1984

Bill Clemente told Plaintiff that Tony Luna was terminated for wastage of time, and that Plaintiff was only supposed to deal with the other shop stewards, Joe Greenwald and Roger Young. Plaintiff did contact Greenwald and Young about his grievance, and they told him that it was a 'dead issue."

April 1984

Roy Goytia told Plaintiff that he was going to be fired soon. That the company has friends in Government, the police force and so on, and that Plaintiff did not know who he was dealing with. Willie Smith told Plaintiff that he was "hot today" and that maybe "he was going to get a fuck from Edna Rangel (an employee of defendant) today".

May 1984

Bill Clemente Told Plaintiff that he was a bad apple that was going to get weeded out. Leo Karpinski told Plaintiff that after Plaintiff was fired from Defendant's employment, he would be very luck to find another job and that Plaintiff didn't need a job because he doesn't "fuck anyway".

ANTHONY GOLUSZEK

SUPREME COURT OF THE UNITED STATES
OFFICE OF THE CLERK
WASHINGTON, DC 20543-0001

April 16, 2007

Antony P. Golluszek
3034 Chgo Road, Apt. 7
S. Chicago, IL 60411

    RE: Anthony P. Goluszek

Dear Mr. Goluszek:

In reply to your letter of submission, received April 10k, 2007, I regret to inform you that the Court is unable to assist you in the matter your present.

Under Article III of the Constitution, the jurisdiction of this Court extends only to the consideration of cases or controversies properly brought before it from lower courts in accordance with federal law and filed pursuant to the Rules of this Court.

Your papers are herewith returned.

Sincerely,
William K. Kuter, Clerk
By:

Clayton R. Higgins, Jr.
(202) 479-3019

Harass Dating   57

Since the following was endorsement of sexual harassment by labor board grievance was a non gross level by Crawford in 1984.

In 1989 Federal district court 86C8412 and 7th Circuit appeal Thomas F Strup Clerk and judges Posner, Flaum and Ripple, Fraud assault and harassment was endorsed.

In 1992 Sargent Folliard Chicago Police not a criminal matter was endorsed too. Supreme Court Clerk Higgins signed also received papers of case believed not be a criminal matter too.

What was said, you can use at work, bars parks and etc. for harassment of persons and assault of person by poking of.

If arrested place bond as soon as possible. Gots a gay jury in a criminal court to present papers to get off.

Then gots civil court for mental damages of being arrested. Get cash award for pain and suffering.

Certificate

Tony Goluszek

FOR YOUR VERY OUTSTANDING
PERFORMANCE
YOU ARE AWARDED:

"One Attaboy"

ONE THOUSAND "ATTABOYS" QUALIFIES YOU TO BE A LEADER OF MEN.

WORK OVERTIME WITH A SMILE, EXPLAIN ASSORTED PROBLEMS

TO MANAGEMENT, AND BE LOOKED UPON AS A LOCAL HERO.

NOTE: ONE "AWSHIT" WIPES THE BOARD CLEAN
AND YOU HAVE TO START ALL OVER AGAIN

1. Publish

LOCAL #714 I. B. T. and _H.P Smith_
(Company)

G R I E V A N C E F O R M

DATE FILED: 2-7-84   (GRIEVANCE # _______)
DATE OF GRIEVANCE: 2-26-84
GRIEVANCE AND FACTS GIVING RISE TO GRIEVANCE: Supervisors Bad
and Discumitve Conduct also written letter.
1. Leo Karpenski charge of out of Plant
without Permission. Lies about work not
being done on #27 machine, which is harrassment
2. Bill Clemete meeting with Ray Goyek in a
harrasment; which he stated Quote " Fuck
in ass about another person is just plain
shop talk", which is Sex
discrimination to self.
SIGNATURE OF EMPLOYEE: _Anthony P. Goluszek_ DEPT. -Maintence
SIGNATURE OF STEWARD: _______

DISPOSITION OF DEPT. SUPERVISOR: Bill Clemete
appologized for statement said
Leo Karpenski refuse to withdraw letter,
and acceptance of my
work performance on #27 machine
which was a Lie and harrassing

SIGNATURE OF DEPT. SUPERVISOR: _______ DATE _______
DATE APPEALED TO STEP 2 OF CONTRACT:

Appeal to JT Webb
because of Personals
Lack of Understanding

(Sex harrass, intimidation & lsay
Solisitation to do
felony X Cimm
Sexual assault)

     ANTHONY GOLUSZEK

H. P. SMITH
DIVISION OF JAMES RIVER CORPORATION
5001 W. 66th Street, Bedford Park, Illinois 60638

February 8, 1984

Mr. Anthony Goluszek
H. P. Smith

Dear Tony:

The grievance you first submitted for Step 2 consideration on February 7, 1984 was by your own statement reviewed by supervision and denied at Step 1 on January 26, 1984.

Given these times, the grievance has not been submitted within the time limits as outlined in Article 10 of the Current Working Agreement. Therefore, the matter you outlined cannot be accepted as a proper grievance and is being returned to you. However, you may feel free to discuss a problem you have with supervision, superintendent, etc.

Very truly yours,

John J. Mietlicki
Industrial Relations Manager

JJM:dlm

cc: W. Clemente
    M. R. Malloy
    J. L. Gibbons
    J. T. Webb
    A. Luna
    H. P. Trendle

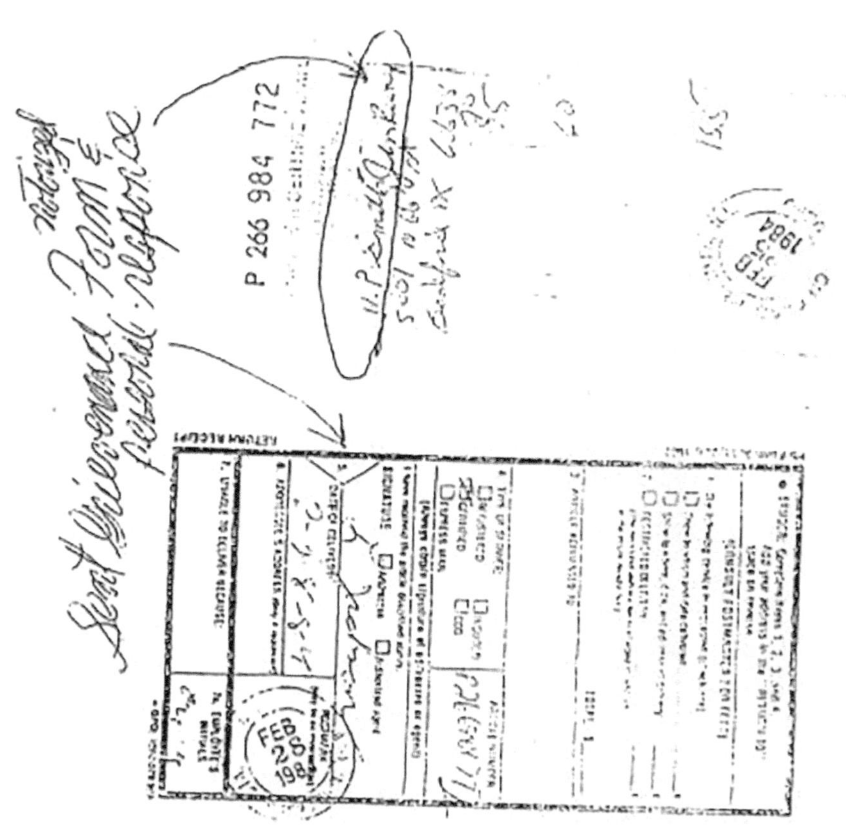

ANTHONY GOLUSZEK

NATIONAL LABOR RELATIONS BOARD

REGION 13

881 Everett McKinley Dirksen Building

219 South Dearborn Street, Chicago, Illinois 60604   Telephone (312) 353- 7171

June 21, 1984

Anthony Goluszek
1239 Vincennes
Chicago Heights, Illinois 60411

> Re: International Brotherhood of
>   Teamsters, Chauffeurs, Warehousemen &
>   Helpers of America, Local 714
>   (N.P. Smith)
>   Case 13-CB-10633

Dear Mr. Goluszek:

The above-captioned case charging a violation under Section 8 of the National Labor Relations Act, as amended, has been carefully investigated and considered.

From the investigation, the evidence does not show that the Union's failure to timely process your grievance rose to the level of gross negligence or that the Union otherwise violated its duty of fair representation in this matter. Office and Professional Employees International Union, Local No. 2, AFL-CIO, 268 NLRB No. 207, (1984). I am, therefore, refusing to issue complaint herein.

Pursuant to the National Labor Relations Board Rules and Regulations, Series 8, as amended, you may obtain a review of this action by filing an appeal with the Acting General Counsel addressed to the Office of Appeals, National Labor Relations Board, Washington, D. C. 20570, and a copy with me. This appeal must contain a complete statement setting forth the facts and reasons upon which it is based. The appeal must be received by the Acting General Counsel in Washington, D. C., by the close of business on July 5, 1984. Upon good cause shown, however, the Acting General Counsel may grant special permission for a longer period within which to file. Any request for extension of time must be submitted to the Office of Appeals in Washington, and a copy of any such request should be submitted to me.

If you file an appeal, please complete the notice forms I have enclosed with this letter and send one copy of the form to each of the other parties. Their names and addresses are listed below. The notice forms should be mailed at the same time you file the appeal, but mailing the notice forms does not relieve you of the necessity for filing the appeal itself with the Acting General Counsel and a copy of the appeal with the Regional Director within the time stated above.

Very truly yours,

Donald J. Crawford
Regional Director

Enclosure
Certified Mail
(Return Receipt Requested)
cc: See Page 2

<table>
<tr><td>CHARGE AGAINST LABOR ORGANIZATION OR ITS AGENTS</td><td>Date Filed
June 6, 1984</td></tr>
</table>

INSTRUCTIONS: File and original and 3 copies of this charge and an additional copy for each organization, each local, and each individual named in Item 1 with the NLRB Regional Director of the Region in which the alleged unfair labor practice occurred or is occurring.

1. LABOR ORGANIZATION OR ITS AGENTS AGAINST WHICH CHARGE IS BROUGHT

a. Name	b. Union Representative to Contact
International Brotherhood of Teamsters, Chauffeurs, Warehousemen & Helpers of America, Local 714	Ralph McClain, B.A.

c. Telephone No.	d. Address (Street, city, state and ZIP code)
242-3215	6815 W. Roosevelt Rd., Berwyn, Il. 60402

e. The above-named organization(s) or its agents has (have) engaged in and is (are) engaging in unfair labor practices within the meaning of section 8(b), subsection(s) __(1)(A)__ (list subsections) of the National Labor Relations Act, and these unfair labor practices are unfair labor practices affecting commerce within the meaning of the Act.

2. Basis of the Charge (be specific as to facts, names, addresses, plants involved, dates, places, etc.)

On or about January, 29, 1984, the above-named labor organization, by its officers and agents, inlcuding steward Tony Luna failed to represent Anthony Goluszek through its negligence of failing to timely file a grievance on behalf of Anthony Goluszek.

3. Name of Employer		4. Telephone No.
N.P. Seith		458-0233

5. Location of Plant Involved (street, city, state and ZIP code)	6. Employer Representative to Contact
5001 W. 66th, Bedford Park, Il. 60638	John Mietllicki

7. Type of Establishment (factory, mine, wholesaler, etc.)	8. Identify Principal Product or Service	9. No. of Workers Employed
Factory	Decals	

10. Full Name of Party Filing Charge

Anthony Goluszek

11. Address of Party Filing Charge (street, city, state and ZIP code)	12. Telephone No.
1239 Vincennes, Chicago Heights, Il. 60411	755-6439

13. DECLARATION

I declare that I have read the above charge and that the statements therein are true to the best of my knowledge and belief.

By _Anthony P. Goluszek_   As Individual
(signature of representative or person making charge)   (title or office, if any)

Address _as above_   _as above_   6/6/84
   (telephone number)   (date)

WILLFULLY FALSE STATEMENTS ON CHARGE CAN BE PUNISHED BY FINE AND IMPRISONMENT
(U.S. CODE, TITLE 18, SECTION 1001)

     ANTHONY GOLUSZEK

CLIENT'S COPY

IN THE UNITED STATES DISTRICT COURT
FOR THE NORTHERN DISTRICT OF ILLINOIS
EASTERN DIVISION

ANTHONY P. GOLUSZEK,	)	
Plaintiff,	)	
v.	)	No. 86 C 8412
H.P. SMITH,	)	
Defendant.	)	

MEMORANDUM OPINION AND ORDER

In this Title VII case, the plaintiff Anthony Goluszek claims that he was the victim of sexual harassment by other males who worked for the defendant H.P. Smith. He also claims that H.P. Smith fired him because (1) he is Polish and (2) in retaliation for his complaining about the sexual harassment. In this opinion, the court addresses the merits of H.P. Smith's motion for summary judgment.

Facts [1]

Anthony Goluszek has never been married nor has he lived anywhere but at his mother's home. According to Goluszek's

---

[1] The parties submitted their statements of uncontested and contested facts. N.D. Ill. Gen. R. 12. Pursuant to local rule and for purposes of the defendant's motion, the court treats as admitted any factual assertion not expressly controverted by the opposing party.

psychiatrist, Goluszek comes from an "unsophisticated background" and has led as "isolated existence" with "little or no sexual experience." Goluszek "blushes easily" and is abnormally sensitive to comments pertaining to sex. Plaintiff's Exhibit ("PX") A.

H.P. Smith is a division of James River Corporation engaged in the business of treating paper with a polyethylene coating for use as freezer wrap and the like. In December of 1976 H.P. Smith hired Goluszek as an electronic maintenance mechanic whose job was to maintain and repair the machines used in production. While he worked at H.P. Smith, Goluszek was represented by Local 714 of the International Brotherhood of Teamsters [2] and his employment was governed by the union's collective bargaining agreement with H.P. Smith. A subsection of Section 11 of that agreement provides that an employee's "[w]illfully creating avoidable waste of time or material" constitutes a just cause for discharge. Goluszek Deposition Exhibit ("Dep. X.") 18a at 22.

Shortly after Goluszek started at H.P. Smith in December of 1976, a number of machine operators questioned him as to why he had no wife or girlfriend and joked that one had to be

---

[2] Local 714 was originally a defendant in this action, but on January 7, 1988 pursuant to a stipulation the court dismissed all claims against the union with prejudice.

married to work there. One year later, the same operators told him that if he could not fix a machine, they would call his "daddy" in. Apparently the operators were referring to Goluszek's supervisor Michael Byczek who, like Goluszek, is of Polish descent. Goluszek reported the latter incident to his night supervisor Cal Adair. Adair responded by using the same remark the operators had used regarding Goluszek's "daddy." In 1978, Adair on one occasion told Goluszek that if Goluszek could not fix a machine he would be sent to a sausage factory. Adair also said Goluszek needed to "get married and get some of that soft pink smelly stuff that's between the legs of a woman." Goluszek responded that Adair should not comment on Goluszek's personal life. PX B.

In the spring of 1979, certain operators told Goluszek he should get married and that he should go out with another employee named Kathy Kristen because she "fucks." Goluszek reported this to Adair whose response was that if Goluszek did not fix a machine they would get "Kathy Kristen to fix Tony." PX B.

Sometime subsequently in 1979, H.P. Smith transferred Goluszek to the day shift. On a number of occasions on this shift, employees driving jeeps threatened to knock Goluszek off of his ladder. Goluszek complained about this practice to Byczek and to the General Manager John Van Buskirk. They assured him 'the matter would be investigated. Goluszek also filed a grievance with Local·714 which the union declined to pursue. He then sent a copy of his grievance to the National Labor Relations Board which in turn directed him to the Occupational Safety and Health Commission. ("OSHA"). After an investigation, OSHA informed Goluszek by letter that it had found no violation and that H. P. Smith was observing appropriate safety measures.

On October 16, 1980, Plant Engineer J. R. Macfarlane issued a warning to Goluszek regarding Goluszek's careless installation of a ballast in a light fixture. Macfarlane warned that continued poor performance would lead to termination.

Subsequently Goluszek requested a meeting which was held on December 4, 1980. Plant Manager Jim Rooney and Byczek were present. Goluszek complained about the Macfarlane reprimand and the danger forklift drivers presented to him. He even threatened court action. A similar meeting was held with Van Buskirk and others on February 27, 1981. Van Buskirk later by letter informed Goluszek that his allegations were without substance and warned that "a continuation of actions on [Goluszek's] part which result in personal unrest, employee antagonism, wastage of company material or time, is sufficient cause for [Goluszek's] termination." Goluszek Dep. X. 10.

H.P. Smith transferred Goluszek back to the night shift sometime in 1981. On that shift, the operators periodically asked Goluszek if he had gotten any "pussy" or had oral sex, showed him pictures of nude women, told him they would get him "fucked," accused him of being gay or bisexual, and made other sex-related comments. The operators also poked him in the buttocks with a stick. Goluszek complained to General Foreman Bill Clemente about the remarks, but Clemente did nothing. Goluszek has admitted that the employees on both shifts talked about sex with one another and used words such as "fuck" in those conversations. He also admits that comments about sex were made that were not directed at him. E.g., Goluszek Dep. at 191-95.

In 1983 and 1984, a number of complaints arose regarding Goluszek's job performance. In May of 1983, Production Foreman Leo Karpinski (who also is Polish) issued a verbal warning to Goluszek because of Goluszek's failure to follow safety procedures and use protective sleeves. As a consequence of his neglect, Goluszek had been burned when working on a defective heater. On January 18, 1984, Karpinski gave Goluszek a written warning for wasting time by being out of the plant without permission on January 12, 1984. [3/] Also in January of 1984 employee Roy Goytia complained to Clemente that Goluszek had

---

[3/] Goluszek appears to believe that Karpinski filed the warning because Goluszek had filed a safety report against Karpinski regarding the latter's procedure for repairing a broken water hose. See PX C.

been trying to get Goytia to complain about Karpinski. On January 26, 1984, Clemente spoke with Goluszek and Goytia at which time Goluszek complained that he was being harassed by employees "out there talking to me about butt fucking in the ass." Goluszek Dep. at 248. Clemente told Goluszek such statements were mere "shop talk." After Goluszek filed a grievance against Clemente, Clemente apologized. The grievance was eventually denied as untimely.

Goluszek's problems continued in April of 1984. On April 10, 1984, Goluszek received a warning for excessive tardiness, his third in three years. On April 11, 1984, Clemente and Karpinski found Goluszek with his feet up on the desk when he was supposed to be looking for a part. H.P. Smith suspended Goluszek for three days and warned that a similar incident would result in termination. Goluszek filed a grievance regarding the April 11 incident, but that grievance was dismissed when he failed to appear at the grievance meeting.

May of 1984 marked the end of Goluszek's employment with H.P. Smith. On May 8, 1984, Clemente issued him another written warning for being late four times in the prior twenty-seven days. On May 9, 1984, Goluszek took six hours to complete a project that normally took one to two. [4] On May 10, 1984,

---

[4] Goluszek attributes the delay to his difficulty in finding a part. <u>See</u> PX C.

 ANTHONY GOLUSZEK

Goluszek admitted that he had not done any work for one and one-half hours. On May 14, 1984, Goluszek was absent from work without an excuse. The next day Goluszek again did nothing for an hour and a half despite being given a work order. Goluszek claims to have been looking for the requisite tools. On May 16, 1984, H.P. Smith suspended Goluszek indefinitely. Eventually H.P. Smith fired Goluszek and Goluszek's grievance was denied. Goluszek admits that the company followed its progressive discipline policy before subjecting him to discharge.

On April 21, 1984, H.P. Smith fired a Hispanic employee named Tony Luna for the same reason it fired Goluszek -- willfully creating avoidable waste of time or material. But unlike Goluszek, Luna prior to his discharge had never been issued a three-day suspension or a final warning that further misconduct would be cause for discharge. H.P. Smith also failed to give Luna a chance to explain his actions. On May 21, 1984, H.P. Smith reinstated Luna.

Finally, some evidence exists that H.P. Smith reacted differently to female claims of sexual harassment than male claims. In a letter dated November 29, 1972, an H.P. Smith supervisor warned an employee regarding the latter's "harassing of a female employee." The letter warned that further harassment would lead to disciplinary action or even discharge. PX E.

Law Offices

CLAUDIA ONEY, P. C.

55 EAST MONROE STREET • SUITE 3420 • CHICAGO, ILLINOIS 60603 • 312-782-1964

Janaury 17, 1989

Mr. Anthony Goluszek
1239 Vincennes Ave.
Chicago Heights, Illinois 60411

Re: Goluszek vs. H.P. Smith

Dear Tony:

As I discussed with you in my office, the judge's ruling in your case was based on her finding that your termination was not due to your complaints of harassment. In other words, the judge found that your discharge was not in retaliation for you making complaints of harassment.

As such, this ruling did not hold that you were not sexually harassed. In fact, the judge described the working conditions under which you worked to be very difficult. She did not contest your testimony of harassment. She simply ruled that even though you may have been harassed, this harassment was not the cause of your discharge.

As you know, the question of whether you are protected under Title VII from the harassment you experienced was not part of the trial, since the judge had earlier ruled that you are not so protected. This is the primary basis on which an appeal would be filed. If the appeals court finds that you are so protected, your case will be remanded for trial on that issue. In that event, a trial will be held where the question of the harassment itself will be litigated. In view of the court's finding of the harassing atmosphere at H.P. Smith, a certain amount of that issue has already been shown. In short, the question is not so much whether you were harassed, but whether you are protected under Title VII from this harassment. That is what appealing your case would answer.

ANTHONY GOLUSZEK

Finally, we had discussed appealing your case and the method of payment in that event. I still await your decision on whether you wish to appeal. Specifically, $2,000.00 payable by March 1, 1989 and $1,500.00 payable by January 1, 1990. These amounts include a petition for hearing by the U.S. Supreme Court if we lose in the Seventh Circuit Court of Appeals. If the U.S. Supreme Court agrees to hear your case we would discuss the fees for that level of appeal when so notified. Your chances of having the case heard by the U.S. Supreme Court are no better than about one in sixteen. Please be aware that a notice of appeal should be filed no later than January 23, 1989.

I also want to thank you for your cooperation and assistance throughout the trial. And, although your sister did not testify I also appreciate her help. I will be waiting for your direction as to whether or not to order the transcripts of Mr. Tony Luna's testimony, Mr. Emil Bohacz's testimony, Mr. Casey Kubecki's testimony and Mr. John Mietlicki's testimony. These witnesses were valuable in establishing the atmosphere of harassment at H.P. Smith. Mr. Bohacz and Mr. Kubecki, in particular will be helpful if we proceed on appeal since they described being sexually harasssed by the company. Mr. Luna and Mr. Mietlicki discribed harassing people sexually so that their testimony will be used by us as well. Again, we will ask the appellate court to find the trial judge to have erred in finding that <u>males cannot harass males under Title VII.</u>

Sincerely,
CLAUDIA ONEY, ESQ.

Claudia Oney

CO/jll

cc:

1239 Vincennes Ave.
Chicago Hts., IL. 60411
(312) 755-6493

RECEIVE
- 1989
THOMAS F. STRUP
CLERK

Dear Sirs:

My sexual harassment case was judged by Judge Ann Williams of U.S. District court, Everett McKinley Dirken Bulding, Chgo., IL. . My Lawyers name was Claudia Oney, 55 E. Monroe St., Ste. number 3420 Chgo., IL. 60603. My file and docket number is 86 C 8412.

My original complaint was at the Judicial Inquiry Board, they refered me to you for complaints against federal judges.

My complaint is that the judge in her summary decision was that only women can be sexually harassed not men.

I had three witnesses that testified in court, Casy Kubicki, Emil Bohas knew of the harassment I was going through. Anthony Luna, my union stewart even knew of harassment and even me being assaulted with a stick while working.

I was rejected help from my union 714 and all of company management of H.P. Smith, and being disciplined while it was going on making the charge of retaliation.

I told the judge by letter, before going to court that I was getting bad references for work which gave me no money to pay for appeals in seveth district court. I got all kinds of job rejecting letters

I gave as evidence all kinds of letters verifing my complainitg. This company was so bad I had to take valium medication while I was working on the job.

I recieved all kinds of threating letters to put up with all kinds of harassment or I wouldbe fired. The company's own memorandum introduced, into evidence of court, tells of there being bad supervisors reputation in June of 1984.

I feel that the judges ruling was so bad to state shes a pervert or was paid off. I know if I was on the streets with this sexual har- assment talk that I would be arr- ested and put away or worse. She makes this misconduct acceptable there by making the charge of federal judges misconduct complaint. Thank you.

Sincerely,

Anthony P. Goluszek

Anthony P. Goluszek

3/30/89	ORDER: Re counsel for Appellant Anthony P. Goluszek's "Letter" advising the court that [illegible] and [illegible] counsel of record for the appellant. The letter in this shall be HELD IN ABEYANCE pending receipt of this filing. [89-1136] [31340-1] (the·y
4/7/89	Filed motion by Claudia Oney [illegible] to [illegible] counsel for the Appellant Anthony P. Goluszek, [illegible] [89-1136] (jcon)
4/11/89	Filed motion by pro se Appellant Anthony P. Goluszek to waive the fee for the transcript. [illegible] [89-1136] (jcon)
4/11/89	ORDER issued GRANTING motion to withdraw as counsel [47016-1] attorney Claudia Oney for Anthony P. Goluszek [89-1136] (jcon)
4/11/89	ORDER: The following briefing schedule is hereby adopted: [89-1136] [31340-1] [illegible] 1. The appellant(s) brief is due on or before 5/11/89 for Anthony P. Goluszek. 2. The appellee(s) brief is due on or before 6/12/89 for H. P. Smith. 3. The reply brief if any is due on or before 6/26/89 for Anthony P. Goluszek. (jcon)
4/25/89	ORDER issued DENYING motion which the court construed as a motion to have the court pay for the cost of preparing the court reporter's transcript for the [illegible] appeal. Appellant may move in the district court for leave to appeal in forma pauperis. See Federal Rule of Appellate Procedure 24. [47848-1] [89-1136] (jcon)
4/27/89	Filed motion by Appellant Anthony [illegible] to [illegible] appeal counsel. [51252-1] [89-1136] [illegible]
4/28/89	The Court, on its own motion, files [illegible] to hold the briefing schedule IN ABEYANCE pending a ruling on appellant's motion for appointment of counsel. [51468-1] [89-1136] [51468-1] (jcon)
7/16/90	ORDER issued DENYING motion to appoint counsel [51242-1] [89-1136] 1. The appellant(s) brief is due on or before 8/17/90 for Anthony P. Goluszek. 2. The appellee(s) brief is due on or before 9/17/90 for H. P. Smith. 3. The reply brief if any is due on [illegible] for Anthony P. Goluszek. (gina)
8/9/90	Appearance form filed by attorney [illegible] (L. Clobben, David B. Ritter for Appellee H. P. Smith. [89-1136] [51468-1] (elsa)
9/26/90	ORDER: Mark Riveria for Appellant Anthony P. Goluszek is directed to [illegible] as to why the appeal should not be dismissed for lack of prosecution pursuant to Circuit Rule 31(e)(2). [89-1136] [31340-1] Response due on or before 10/10/90 for Mark Riveria. (mk)
10/10/90	Filed response to order to [illegible] by Mark Riveria for Appellant Anthony P. Goluszek. [89-1136] [51468-1] (jcon)

United States Court of Appeals

For the Seventh Circuit
Chicago, Illinois 60604

January 30, 1991

Before

Hon. RICHARD A. POSNER, Circuit Judge

Hon. JOEL M. FLAUM, Circuit Judge

Hon. KENNETH F. RIPPLE, Circuit Judge

No. 89-1136	) Appeal from the United States) District Court for the

ANTHONY P. GOLUSZEK,
    Plaintiff-Appellant,
    v.
H. P. SMITH,
    Defendant-Appellee.
	) Northern District of Illinois
	) Eastern Division
	) No. 86 C 8412
	) Judge Ann Claire Williams
	)

As of this date, there has been no response to this court's rule to show cause of October 18, 1990. Accordingly, pursuant to that rule and CR 31(c)(2),

IT IS ORDERED that this appeal is DISMISSED for want of prosecution.

CITY OF CHICAGO / DEPARTMENT OF POLICE
1121 South State Street
Chicago, Illinois 60605

(312) 744-4000

Text Telephones
(312) 922-1414 (24 Hrs. & Emergency)
(312) 744-8006 (Business Hours)

October 21, 1992

Richard M. Daley, Mayor
Matt L. Rodriguez, Superintendent of Police

Anthony P. Goluszek
1239 Vincennes Ave.
Chicago Heights, Illinois 60411

Dear Mr. Goluszek:

The Chicago Police Department has received your mailgram dated August 12, 1992. Your correspondence was forwarded to me for initial investigation. After speaking to you by phone on October 20, 1992, I was able to determine that your complaint regards the conduct of several attorneys who participated in a federal court hearing before Judge Ann Williams.

In your conversation, you related your displeasure with the actions and comments of your attorney during your court appearance that involved allegations of sexual harassment and a workman's compensation claim.

Although this case was heard in Chicago, Illinois, there does not appear to be any criminal matter requiring the attention of the Chicago Police Department.

I am, however, providing you with the addresses and phone numbers of two other agencies that may be able to assist you in pressing for any civil or administrative remedies that you may seek. They are:

Attorney Registration and Discipline Commission of the Supreme Court of Illinois
203 N. Wabash
Chicago, Illinois
346-0690

Legal Assistance Foundation
343 S. Dearborn
Chicago, Illinois
341-1070

Sgt. Thomas Folliard
Bureau of Investigative Services
Chicago Police Department

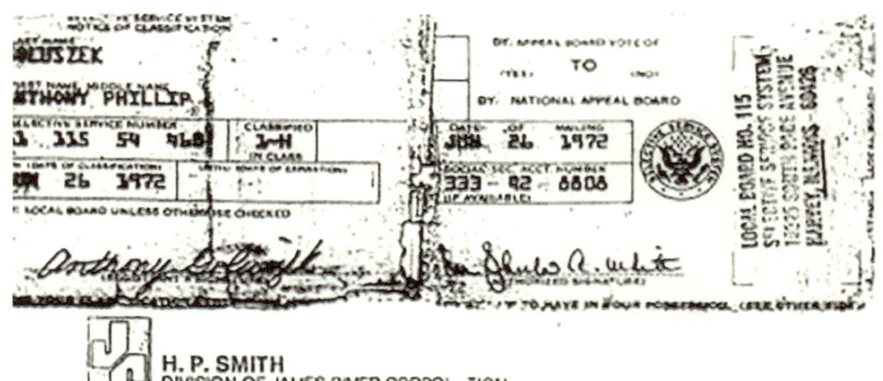

H. P. SMITH
DIVISION OF JAMES RIVER CORPORATION
5001 W. Sixth-Sixth St., Bedford Park, IL 60638 (312) 458-0777

January 23, 1984

Mr. Anthony P. Goluszek
1239 Vincennes Ave.
Chicago Heights, IL   60411

Dear Tony:

As you know, H.P. Smith has just completed another year of improved
safety performance. Both the Chicago and Iowa City facilities achieved
their respective 1983 safety objectives with seven and three OSHA
recordable injuries. You, as an individual, played a significant role
in the total team that provided this achievement by not experiencing
a doctor treated case in 1983.

Our safety program included numerous policies, procedures, and practices designed to prevent injuries. These include such activities as
monthly safety inspections, fire brigades, accident investigations,
safe operating procedures, etc. More important, it includes the
individual activities of all the employees. It has been through your
efforts and safe work practices that H.P. Smith has been able to
achieve our safety objectives for 1983.

I compliment you and thank you for your interest in our safety program
which allowed you to have an injury-free year, and know we will receive
your support in our safety program during 1984.

Sincerely,

H. P. SMITH

J. L. Rooney
Vice President/General Manager

JLR:ll

H P SMITH PAPER CO   5001 WEST SIXTY SIXTH STREET, CHICAGO, IL 66638 U.S.A.   PHONE 312 458 0777   TELEX 79-4343

July 26, 1983

Mr. Anthony Goluszek
H. P. Smith Paper Co.

Dear Mr. Goluszek:

The grievance you submitted on June 30, 1983 was reviewed in a
Second Step Meeting held on July 12, 1983.

The grievance review indicates that there has not been a violation
of the Current Working Agreement, therefore, the grievance is denied.

Work assignments which you call "electrician work" will continue to
be given to you just as they have been given to you and others in
your job classification in the past. It is worth noting that you
have successfully completed these assignments in the past, so your
claim that you are not qualified in these areas is most difficult
to understand. Employees in the Electronics Maintenance Man Job
classification have for a long period performed what you call
"electrician work" such as bending conduit, pulling wires, installing
switches or motors as well as periodically troubleshooting solid
state circuitry.

This letter is a rewrite of the letter given you on July 13, 1983.
The final paragraph was deleted pursuant to a grievance settlement.

Very truly yours,

H. P. SMITH PAPER CO.

John J. Mietlicki
Administrative Manager

JJM:kg

cc: J. L. Rooney
    J. R. Macfarlane
    C. Rodriguez
    M. P. Trendle

IN THE UNITED STATES DISTRICT COURT
NORTHERN DISTRICT OF ILLINOIS
EASTERN DIVISION

ANTHONLY GOLUSZEK,   )
)
              Plaintiff,   )
)   No. 86 C 8412
         v.   )
)   Chicago, Illinois
H.P. SMITH, et al.   )   December 2, 1988
)   2:00 p.m.
              Defendants.   )   Trial

TRANSCRIPT OF PROCEEDINGS

BEFORE THE HONORABLE ANN C. WILLIAMS

APPEARANCES:

For Plaintiff: MS. CLAUDIA ONEY
                            MR. MARK D. RIVERA
                            55 East Monroe Street
                            Suite 3420
                            Chicago, Illinois 60603

For the Defendants: MAYER, BROWN & PLATT, by
                            MR. JAMES W. GLADDEN, JR.
                            MR. DAVID B. RITTER
                            190 South LaSalle Street
                            Chicago, Illinois 60603

Court Reporter: Valarie M. Harris
                            Official Court Reporter
                            219 South Dearborn Street
                            Room 1928
                            Chicago, Illinois 60604
                            (312) 435-6891

                  ANTHONY GOLUSZEK

Luna - direct

1   A   It was March 1978, I believe.

2   Q   And do you remember the position into which you were hired?

3   A   I was hired as utility.

4   Q   And how long did you stay in that position?

5   A   It was a matter of a couple of months, and then I got a bid

6   for an operator.

7   Q   Okay. And how long did you stay in the operator's posi-

8   tion?

9   A   For the duration of my employment there.

10   Q   And could you describe your duties as an operator?

11   A   Well, would run their primary machines, which would coat

12   paper.

13   Q   Okay. Were you also a member of a union?

14   A   Yes, Teamsters 714.

15   Q   Other than the position of operator at H.P. Smith, did you

16   have any other -- were you actively engaged in any other

17   position with H.P. Smith?

18   A   I was a union steward.

19   Q   And when were you the union steward?

20   A   From about 1980 until about 1986. A little before 1986.

21   Q   Could you tell us what a union steward does?

22   A   Well, they would go to meetings with the company and work

23   out differences, you know, problems between the union and the

24   company, and they would also be there to protect employees.

25   Q   And how many of these meetings did you attend in all the

1   Q   Do you recall what Tony Goluszek said during that

2   meeting?

3   A   Not really.

4   Q   Do you recall what Bill Clemente said during that

5   meeting?

6   A   Bill stated that Ray was angry at Tony. And Ray was

7   doing most of the talking, and Bill was kind of sitting

8   there, and then Bill told Ray to calm down and, you know,

9   let's get to the bottom of this and pretty much he said,

10 well, if you can't be -- you guys can't be fighting. Let's,

11 you know, go back out there. We've got a job to do. Let's

12 go out there and do it.

13 Q   Do you recall at that meeting Bill Clemente saying that

14 statement such as fucking in the ass about another person is

15 just plain "shop talk"?

16   MR. GLADDEN: Your Honor, he's leading the witness.

17   THE COURT: Sustained.

18   MR. RIVERA: Your Honor, it's set out in the

19 grievance form. It was signed by Tony Goluszek.

20   THE COURT: Well, then refer him to the grievance

21 form and have him read from that. You were leading.

22   MR. RIVERA: Okay, Judge.

23 BY MR. RIVERA:

24 Q   Now, you signed this grievance form, is that correct?

25 A   Right.

1   Q   And when you signed the grievance form you -- that was

2   your signature attesting to what was stated in that grievance

3   form?

4   A   Well, pretty much. My signature is here for policy,

5   because they won't accept a grievance unless it's signed by

6   the steward. So I didn't write this grievance, but I did

7   sign it so the man was -- he was feeling grieved. He wanted

8   to file a grievance, and in order to have a meeting I have to

9   sign this.

10   Q   What's said on the grievance form as to what Bill

11   Clemente said, do you recall that being said?

12   A   Yes, because that was a big thing. Everybody picked on

13   Tony.

14   MR. GLADDEN: Your Honor, I have to object.

15   THE COURT: Sustained. Disregard it. Strike it.

16   MR. RIVERA: Strike it as to everybody picking on

17   Tony?

18   THE COURT: Yes. Yes.

19   MR. RIVERA: But as to yes --

20   THE COURT: That portion can stand.

21   MR. RIVERA: Okay. Thank you, Judge.

22   BY MR. RIVERA:

23   Q   Now, after this meeting, did you have any other

24   conversation with Tony Goluszek regarding this grievance form

25   and that meeting?

1   I think that was there, but I just can't remember who was

2   there.

3   BY MR. RIVERA:

4   Q   Okay. And can you tell us what was said?

5   A   Well, mainly we were asking him about girlfriends and

6   stuff, and it's kind -- they were asking him if he had any

7   sex with any girlfriends, and he was like saying no at the

8   time, and then they started getting to him about like

9   homosexual relationships about, you know, screwing in the

10   ass, stuff like that.

11   Q   Now, Mr. Luna, I want you to be, as best you can, to

12   tell us exactly what was said. Now, was that the phrase that

13   they used: Tony, have you ever had sex with a woman? What

14   was the language that they used?

15   A   No, they would talk about Tony, did you ever fuck a

16   girl. Did you ever, you know, did you ever fuck a girl in

17   the ass and then like Corbett, said, well, did you ever fuck

18   a guy in the ass, and he was like kind of like, you know, I

19   don't talk like that. That's not my kind of thing.

20   Q   That's Tony's reaction?

21   A   That's Tony's reaction.

22   Q   Was there any other physical reaction to Tony?

23   A   Well, later on, like a few minutes later, Tony started

24   working on the machine. He had to go check the hoist and he

25   was up on the ladder and Al came by with a broom and then

           Anthony Goluszek

1   stuck it in his butt and Tony like almost fell off the ladder

2   in shock.

3   Q   Do you recall anything else that Tony Goluszek did in

4   response to that?

5   A   Well, he told me at that time that's he not like that

6   and that, you know, people were actually bothering him.

7   Q   Were you ever one of them?

8   A   At first, yes. I was like one of them. We just goofed

9   around with him and have fun, but then he told me it bothers

10 him.

11 Q   And what did you do then?

12 A   So I stopped and I didn't, you know, didn't harass him

13 or nothing like that. I tried not to, you know. And if I

14 did, I told him, Tony, I'm sorry. I don't mean it like that,

15 you know, if he thought I was wrong, you know.

16 Q   Now, after Al Corbett stuck him with a stick, did you

17 see what Al Corbett did after that or said?

18 A   No. That's all I can remember, comes real clear with

19 him standing on the ladder and him going like this with the

20 broom.

21 Q   Any other occasion where you witnessed this?

22 A   Well, anytime we got by the machine and we called for

23 maintenance and we need an electrician, Tony would come over

24 and usually we'd get a couple of guys and get around and

25 start talking about this stuff.

```
1    Q    We had a chance to review today a copy of your
2    personnel file that was provided to me by H.P. Smith.  Is
3    that the address and telephone number that appear on your
4    employee personnel data change that was in this file?
5    A    Which document?
6    Q    It's the employee personnel data change.  Your
7    telephone and address appear in that file?
8    A    Yes, it is signed by me.  That was the document that
9    was signed by me when H.P. was sold to James Rivers.
10   Q    Thank you.  Would you please give the Court a brief
11   description of your employment background and educational
12   background?
13   A    Educationally I graduated from Loyola in 1969 with a
14   bachelor's of arts, and graduated in 1976 from Loyola with a
15   master's in business administration in personnel industrial
16   relations.  Been in the human resources area a little over
17   19 years.  10 years of which I worked for H.P. Smith, then
18   Phillips Products, which were then subsidiaries of Phillips
19   Petroleum.  I worked for several other companies in varying
20   capacities.
21   Q    After you left H.P. Smith where did you go to work?
22   A    I worked for a period of about five months with Keith
23   Ross & Associates.
24   Q    And after that?
25   A    I worked a year at the Illinois Local Labor Relations
```

1   MS. ONEY: Your Honor, I have one witness who's

2   been waiting since about 2 or 3. I don't think he'll take

3   long. We have -- I've received a stipulation from counsel

4   as to an exhibit that will substantially cut down the --

5   THE COURT: All right. Bring him in.

6   MS. ONEY: I've got a baby-sitting problem, so if

7   you want to stop, but I think we can do this quickly.

8   THE COURT: Well, bring him in. We'll see.

9   I'll recess if we can't.

10   MS. ONEY: Okay.

11   (Witness sworn.)

12   JOHN MIETLICKI, PLAINTIFF'S WITNESS, FIRST DULY SWORN

13   DIRECT EXAMINATION

14   BY MS. ONEY:

15   Q   Please state your name for the record.

16   A   John Mietlicki.

17   Q   Where do you reside?

18   A   3510 West 66th Street, Chicago.

19   THE COURT: Would you spell your last name?

20   THE WITNESS: M-i-e-t-l-i-c-k-i.

21   BY MS. ONEY:

22   Q   How long have you lived at that address?

23   A   Approximately 14 years.

24   Q   What is your telephone number?

25   A   776-8088.

1   Board.

2   Q   And after that?

3   A   And subsequent to that I worked two years, nine months

4   at Blue Cross/Blue Shield of Illinois.

5   Q   All right. Thank you. When did you leave your

6   employment at R.P. Smith?

7   A   April of 1984.

8   Q   All right.

9   MS. ONEY: May I approach the witness?

10   THE COURT: Yes.

11 BY MS. ONEY:

12 Q   I'm showing you a document marked Plaintiff's Exhibit

13 No. 72.

14   MS. ONEY: Your Honor doesn't have a copy of this,

15 but I'm going to tender this to you as soon as the witness

16 identifies it. This has been stipulated to.

17 BY MS. ONEY:

18 Q   Do you recognize that document?

19   THE COURT: All right. It will be admitted.

20   (Plaintiff's Exhibit No. 72 was received in evidence.)

21   THE WITNESS: I have not previously seen the

22 document. It wasn't addressed to me. I didn't get a copy.

23 BY MS. ONEY:

24 Q   But you read it today. Is that right?

25 A   Yes, I have.

1   Q   And do you have -- are the facts as they are set out in

2   that document approximately correct?

3   A   I believe as a transcript of the interview that took

4   place on April 6th, they are correct. They're essentially

5   correct.

6   Q   And the items set out in that document, do they -- what

7   do they represent?

8   A   They represent an interview between James Rooney and

9   myself on April 6th.

10   Q   And just very briefly, the subject matter of that

11   interview?

12   A   Issues, issues involving alleged sexual harassment

13   that -- feeling was that there was a discussion on my part,

14   things that I did that constituted alleged sexual

15   harassment.

16   Q   And what was the result of that interview?

17   A   I resigned.

18   MS. ONRY: Your Honor, this is the Court's copy of

19   this.

20   BY MS. ONRY:

21   Q   Did you believe yourself to have engaged in sexual

22   harassment?

23   A   No, I did not.

24   Q   All right. Were you familiar with an employee while

25   you were at H.P. Smith named Tony Golunszak?

1   A   Yes.

2   Q   Would you please describe your contact you remember

3   with Tony Goluszek?

4   A   Tony was an electronics maintenance man. I had mostly

5   had dealings with him in grievance issues. There were other

6   times when I would walk through the plant and he and I would

7   talk.

8   Q   Do you remember Tony making complaints when you were

9   employed at H.P. Smith?

10   A   Tony, Tony complained about a lot of things during the

11   period of time I was there.

12   Q   What do you remember him complaining about?

13   A   Well, he complained of -- on several occasions of while

14   he was performing work on a ladder some of the forklift

15   drivers coming too close and attempting to hit him and knock

16   him off. He indicated he was afraid of that. He complained

17   of a procedure that required him to go up on a high-bay

18   warehouse and work on the crane that was about 60 feet in

19   the air. He felt the procedure to do the work up there was

20   unsafe. And he complained of a lot of different things. He

21   said that he was being harassed by the guys in the

22   maintenance department, the people on the floor.

23   Q   Did he specify the kind of harassment?

24   A   Initially, no. He claimed that the people on the floor

25   used to kid him, and it was a lot of different people. He

1   never really mentioned any -- any names specifically, but

2   they would kid him about a lot of things.

3   Q   And when did he first report this kidding to you?

4   A   I couldn't precisely say, but I know it was subsequent

5   to the time that James Rivers acquired H.P. Smith.

6   Q   When did James Rivers acquire H.P. Smith?

7   A   I believe it was October -- mid-October of '83.

8   Q   And what action did you take when he reported this

9   kidding to you?

10   A   Well, he complained about a number of things

11   specifically on the harassment. I did not investigate it,

12   per se, but advised Jim MacFarlane who was the maintenance

13   superintendent that Tony was complaining again about a

14   number of things and maybe --

15   Q   Did you have a meeting with Mr. MacFarlane?

16   A   I think I -- I don't know that it was a formal -- ...

17   it was a discussion. I stopped him and said Tony was --

18   Q   When did that occur?

19   A   It was shortly after Tony -- Tony had mentioned to me

20   about --

21   Q   At the end of '83?

22   A   Possibly.

23   Q   And what was said?

24   A   Pardon me?

25   Q   What was said? What did Jim MacFarlane say to you

1

2   I hereby certify that the above-entitled matter is

3   true and correct.

4

5

6

7   ___________________________   3-10-92

8   Reporter   Date

9

10

11

12   ___________________________   3/10/92

     Official Reporter   Date

1   A   Yes.

2   Q   What's the policy, if you would please summarize it,

3   regarding making complaints directly to the company?

4   A   Basically it's --

5   THE COURT: Excuse me. Counsel, it's in the

6   document. I have the document. There's no need for him to

7   read the document.

8   BY MS. ONRY:

9   Q   All right. Did you consider this particular policy in

10 your capacity as industrial relations manager as something

11 that would supplement the union grievance procedure?

12 A   It was an open-door communications policy, and any

13 employee was not prevented from utilizing this procedure

14 without talking to your supervisor about a problem, and they

15 could certainly do that apart from actually filing a formal

16 grievance and it was commonly done that way.

17 Q   Did you consider the -- you were familiar with the

18 union contract?

19 A   Yes.

20 Q   Is that correct?

21 A   Yes.

22 Q   Did you consider it to cover an employee who had a

23 problem with sexual harassment?

24 A   It could. Actually the contract covered any

25 legitimate -- any problem that an employee wished to grieve

1   supporting and implementing this policy."

2   Q   Do you think that policy applied to Tony Goluszek while

3   you were the industrial relations manager?

4   A   It was a policy that applied to everybody at the

5   company.

6   Q   Was it followed regarding Tony Goluszek?

7   A   If Tony Goluszek was an employee --

8   Q   Pardon me?

9   A   If Tony Goluszek was an employee it would have applied

10   to him the same way as any other employee.

11   MS. ONRY: May I approach the witness?

12   THE COURT: Yes.

13   MS. ONRY: No. 70. This has already been

14   admitted.

15   BY MS. ONRY:

16   Q   Would you identify that for the record, please?

17   A   It's the employee communications procedure that was put

18   out under John VanBuskirk's signature who was then president

19   of H.P. Smith.

20   Q   Did you assist in preparing that?

21   A   I was involved. Really I didn't write it. Again this

22   was -- a lot that came out of Phillips Corp. that went into

23   this. This was pretty much a procedure that was implemented

24   company wide.

25   Q   Your name is mentioned, isn't it?

1   Q   The portion concerning harassment, did you write that

2   portion?

3   A   This was basically the policy that had been issued

4   through Phillips Petroleum Company, that we were all the --

5   the personnel managers and industrial relations managers

6   were advised -- were enforced at subsidiary units. You want

7   me to read it or --

8   Q   Any way you want to describe the policy.

9   A   Well, I'll just read it. It's easier. "Phillips

10   Petroleum Company is committed to maintaining a work

11   environment with respect to privacy and dignity of the

12   individual. Physical or verbal harassment of employees or

13   applicants for employment is incompatible with that

14   principle and with acceptable job performance. Harassment

15   includes any conduct that has the purpose of or effect of

16   unreasonably interfering with an individual's work

17   performance or creating an intimidating, hostile and

18   offensive working environment. Inappropriate jokes, slurs

19   tricks, name calling, sexual advancements or comments can

20   constitute harassment.

21   The company's internal communications procedure

22   provides for all employees the avenue through which problems

23   such as harassment can be reported and addressed without

24   fear of reprisal. All employees of Phillips Petroleum

25   Company and subsidiary companies are accountable for

1   manager at H.P. Smith did you ever have occasion to deal

2   with any charges of discrimination?

3   A   Yes, we did have charges filed, handicap discrimination

4   charges and others.

5   Q   Did you have a policy, or were you aware of EEO rules

6   and regulations regarding retaining documents?

7   A   Other than the fact that if a charge was filed we amass

8   all the documents relative to the specific charge or medical

9   records, whatever the case might be, and retain them in the

10   discrimination charge file.

11   THE COURT: Is that about it, counsel?

12   MS. ONEY: Very very close, yes.

13   THE COURT: How long do you think your cross will

14   be? I just want to know if you'll be able to do it in a few

15   minutes or whether we'll have the witness back.

16   MR. GLADDEN: My guess is I can get done in five

17   minutes.

18   MS. ONEY: Your Honor, may I approach the witness?

19   THE COURT: You may.

20   BY MS. ONEY:

21   Q   Exhibit No. 68, would you please identify this for the

22   record?

23   A   This was a notice that was posted at H.P. Smith under

24   my signature regarding access to employee exposure of

25   medical records and harassment.

ANTHONY GOLUSZEK

1   general comments such as that.

2   Q   How many complaints did you hear from Tony directly

3   during the year 1984 concerning sex talk on the factory

4   floor?

5   A   I guess apart from the, you know, my awareness into

6   this grievance, there might have been one other occasion

7   when he mentioned it.

8   Q   Did you ever take any action about this alleged sexual

9   harassment during the year 1984?

10   A   I was only there for under four months. I did not take

11   any -- that was basically what I passed out to the main

12   superintendent.

13   Q   Did you ever have a meeting with J.T. Webb concerning

14   this alleged sexual harassment by Tony?

15   A   I don't know that I had a meeting. I guess I had a

16   discussion. I mentioned it to him that Tony had been by

17   complaining about this, and he indicated, yeah, he was

18   aware, because Tony had stopped him.

19   Q   And did you and he make any effort to resolve this

20   problem or was there --

21   A   I didn't question it. It was just a mention. It was

22   just a mention in passing that Tony had been by and

23   mentioned it to me and the issue of the grievance. That was

24   it. It wasn't any kind of a formal discussion.

25   Q   While you were in your position as industrial relations

1   specifically recall.

2   Q   Do you remember any discussions involving Tony's claim

3   of sexual harassment subsequent to returning that grievance

4   to him?

5   A   With Tony?

6   Q   Yes.

7   A   And Carlos?

8   Q   With Mr. Luna or Mr. Rodriguez.

9   A   With Tony Luna or Carlos Rodriguez?

10   Q   That's correct.

11   A   I really can't recall. I might have mentioned

12   something to them, because they were really the responsible

13   stewards on the shift. And I said, you know, I'm returning

14   the grievance. It might have been kind of like that. I

15   can't specifically -- it wasn't a formalized meeting.

16   Q   Now, you received complaints from Tony Goluszek during

17   the year 1984 when you would encounter him on a one to one

18   basis. Is that correct?

19   A   Every once in a while if he'd see me and when I'd be

20   walking through the plant he, you know, he'd make comments

21   to me that they're at it again or they're doing -- I

22   couldn't really categorize them in any particular way, but

23   typically he would stop me at times, and tell me about

24   problems he was having or there were -- I know he said that

25   they were picking on him again for not doing his job or

1 vice president of manufacturing who was involved again with

2 myself and all the parties. So it was, you know, really the

3 next step in the process except it involved that

4 manufacturing head.

5 Q   The Step 3 decision maker in 1984 would be whom?

6 A   In 1984 it would have been at that point J. Webb,

7 because he was vice president of manufacturing.

8   MS. ONEY: At that time, Your Honor, may I

9 approach the witness?

10   THE COURT: Yes.

11 BY MS. ONEY:

12 Q   Do you remember this grievance, Mr. Mietlicki?

13   THE COURT: Which is which document?

14   MS. ONEY: I'm sorry. No. 4, Judge.

15   THE WITNESS: Yes, I recall the grievance.

16 BY MS. ONEY:

17 Q   Did you conduct any investigation into that document?

18 A   No, I don't believe that there was any investigation at

19 all conducted into it, because of the fact that the

20 grievance was not filed on a timely basis and was returned

21 to the grievant.

22 Q   Did you have a meeting subsequent to returning that

23 document to the grievant with the union stewards, Tony Luna

24 and Carlos Rodriguez?

25 A   I might have had a discussion with them. I can't

1   someone had disciplinary action specifically, or really

2   could be any other action by supervision, management, if, in

3   fact, something was done, and the employee felt he had a

4   legitimate grievance, a grievance was filed and first heard

5   with the supervisor and the superintendent.

6   Q   That's step one.

7   A   That's step one, right. And if, in fact, a grievance

8   was denied at that point then it was brought to me, and said

9   that we want to proceed to the next step. That's when I got

10   involved, and typically a meeting was scheduled with the

11   supervisor, superintendent and myself, the grieving party,

12   the steward, and we had a meeting to sit down and basically

13   rehash the issue again.

14   Q   And who would make the decision after this rehash?

15   A   I would make the decision. Of course, it would be made

16   after discussion again with the superintendent, the

17   supervisor if, in fact, it happened at times in Step 2 of

18   the grievance that we felt the action that was taken was

19   inappropriate; it might have been reduced or eliminated.

20   Q   But you signed the letters?

21   A   Yes, I did. I issued that step of the grievance, and

22   if the grieving party did not agree with that decision we

23   went on to the next step.

24   Q   At the Step 3 level, who would make the decision?

25   A   That was -- well, it was generally the plant manager,

1   and --

2   A   He said he'd check into it.

3   Q   Now, you were personnel manager at that point, right,

4   isn't that basically --

5   A   I was industrial relations manager. They're basically

6   the same thing.

7   Q   They are basically the same thing.

8   Did you ever see any warning letters written or any

9   action at all taken by Jim MacFarlane?

10   A   Relative to what?

11   Q   On the issue of Tony's complaints.

12   A   I don't recall that I've ever seen any documentation

13   like that.

14   Q   Would letters like that be copied to you as personnel

15   manager, or would it be sent to the personnel department?

16   A   If, in fact, it was formal disciplinary action we made

17   it a policy that formal disciplinary action should be sent

18   to us for insertion into the employee's file, yes, if it was

19   formal disciplinary action.

20   Q   Do you know whether or not MacFarlane did anything?

21   A   I have no knowledge whether he did anything.

22   Q   Would you please describe the personnel policies at

23   H.P. Smith regarding union grievances? What's the -- at

24   what part of that process did you become involved?

25   A   I would become involved in Step 2 of the grievance. If

Anthony T. Goluszek
3034 Chgo. Rd. Apt 7
S.C.H., IL, 60411

Supreme Court
1 First St. N.E.
Washington, D.C. USA.

~~Dear Sirs.:~~

As far as I am Concern
I won in the 7th circuit
because they did not
respond to my Complaint
(with 7th circuits)
about Fed. Judges and the
diaries of the 7th circuit.
I could go to your court,
just tell me time and date
to apear.

46
32

RECEIVED
JAN 0 3 2007
OFFICE OF THE CLERK
SUPREME COURT, U.S.

Sincerely
Anthony T. Goluszek

ANTHONY GOLUSZEK

3034 Chgo Hy Apt.7
So, Chgo. Hts
Ill, 60411

Mr, Higgins
Supreme Court
1 First St, N.E
Washington D.C., USA

Dear Sirs;

If the 7th circuit letter was not done right, they would not put seal on it. Must be acceptable at Supreme court and 7th to harass; rope and fraud.

Sincerely

Anthony P. Olegel

(708) 833 5049

1 letters total 21

Subscribed and sworn to before me

this 24th day of JANUARY 2007
at South Chicago Heights, County of Cook,
state of Illinois.

Notary Public

Official Seal
Wanda Morehead
Notary Public State of Illinois
My Commission Expires 06/15/07

Anthony Goluszek
24473
8/17/07

Mr. Goluszek is seen today in a fifteen minute medication check. He says he has been off
of the Tegretol now for quite awhile.   I confronted him again that not only do I think he
needs the Tegretol for his emotions and moods but I also think he needs it for the seizure
that he had. He says he felt the medicine was just too much on his liver even though no
one told him in any kind of blood test that he was having any issues with his liver.   He
also wants to cut the Paxil to 10 mg per day because he feels the 20 mg per day is too
strong also.   He denies any intention of harming himself or anyone else. He denies any
hallucinations. He denies any paranoia. He has become much more compulsive with the
obsession about his prior sexual harassment lawsuit that ended his working career. He
still obsessively is trying to send the paperwork to different places even different states
trying to get someone to take the case to refile all of the motions.   He seems to take in
stride though when people tell him there is really nothing they can do because of how
long ago this all transpired.   His sister is now living with him so at least someone is there
keeping an eye on him just in case he were to have a seizure. He is not driving. He has
not had anything that even resembles a seizure he says. Affect is bright. He is interacting
with friend and going out on a daily basis. Even the jerking movements in his muscles
that he has always had since I met him, seem to be doing a little bit better.   Sleep and
appetite are fine.   He says he is very consistently eating a better diet.

Assessment
Chronic Schizophrenia
Obsessive Compulsive Disorder

Treatment Plan:
I did agree he could decrease Paxil to 10 mg and he agreed he would go back to the
Tegretol 200 mg q am and 400 mg nightly to make sure he had no chance of having a
seizure. He will return in two months for medication monitoring. He will call in the
interim if any problems arise and agreed with the recommendation for today.

Mary E. Belford MD
MEB:kjm

Luna - direct

1   THE COURT: All right. You may take the stand.

2   MR. RIVERA: We'd like to call Tony -- Anthony Luna.

3 (Witness sworn.)

4   ANTONIO LUNA, PLAINTIFF'S WITNESS, DULY SWORN

5   DIRECT EXAMINATION

6 BY MR. RIVERA:

7 Q   Could you state your name for the record, please?

8 A   Antonio Luna, Jr.

9   THE COURT REPORTER: Could you spell your name,

10 please?

11   THE WITNESS: L-u-n-a.

12 BY MR. RIVERA:

13 Q   Mr. Luna, where do you live?

14 A   I live at 10330 South 82nd Avenue in Palos Hills.

15 Q   And how old are you?

16 A   I'm 29.

17 Q   And how is it that you come to appear before this Court

18 today?

19 A   I was subpoenaed for the plaintiff.

20 Q   Mr. Luna, could you just give us a brief outline of your

21 educational background starting with high school and going to

22 any post high school education?

23 A   Okay. I graduated from Oak Lawn Community High School in

24 January 1977, and I attended Moraine Valley Community College

25 for about a year. And then I was off -- I quit school for

1 about ten years, nine years, and I went back to DeVry, and I

2 got a diploma.

3 Q   And while you were at high school, was there any specific

4 area of concentration in which you concentrated?

5 A   Automotive technology.

6 Q   And when you went to one year in college right after high

7 school, was there a specific area of study that you concen-

8 trated it?

9 A   Automotive technology.

10 Q   Now, after you left college after the one year, what did

11 you do?

12 A   I went to work for H.P. Smith.

13 Q   And how long did you work for H.P. Smith?

14 A   It was about eight years, I think, close to nine.

15 Q   And then what did you do after you left H.P. Smith?

16 A   I started with Illinois Bell.

17 Q   And you said you went to college at what time? You went

18 back to college between what?

19 A   In 1984, July 1984 I went back to college.

20 Q   Until?

21 A   Until 1986.

22 Q   And did you state the colleges you went to?

23 A   Moraine Valley College.

24 Q   No, the second college.

25 A   No. I just went to Moraine Valley. Then I went to DeVry.

ANTHONY GOLUSZEK

Luna – direct

1 Q   And what did you study at DeVry?

2 A   Electronic technology.

3 Q   Are you now employed?

4 A   Yes, I am.

5 Q   In what?

6 A   Illinois Bell.

7 Q   What do you do there?

8 A   I'm a central office technician. I run their switch.

9 Q   Okay. Do you recall the date that you were hired for H.P.

10 Smith?

11 A   It was March 1978, I believe.

12 Q   And do you remember the position into which you were hired?

13 A   I was hired as utility.

14 Q   And how long did you stay in that position?

15 A   It was a matter of a couple of months, and then I got a bid

16 for an operator.

17 Q   Okay. And how long did you stay in the operator's posi-

18 tion?

19 A   For the duration of my employment there.

20 Q   And could you describe your duties as an operator?

21 A   Well, would run their primary machines, which would coat

22 paper.

23 Q   Okay. Were you also a member of a union?

24 A   Yes, Teamsters 714.

25 Q   Other than the position of operator at H.P. Smith, did you

1   have any other -- were you actively engaged in any other

2   position with H.P. Smith?

3   A   I was a union steward.

4   Q   And when were you the union steward?

5   A   From about 1980 until about 1986. A little before 1986.

6   Q   Could you tell us what a union steward does?

7   A   Well, they would go to meetings with the company and work

8   out differences, you know, problems between the union and the

9   company, and they would also be there to protect employees.

10 Q   And how many of these meetings did you attend in all the

11 years that you were a steward?

12 A   I'd say hundreds of them.

13 Q   How many grievances did you pursue while you were a union

14 steward?

15 A   Probably hundreds. It might not be that many, but it was

16 quite a bit.

17 Q   Now, generally could you describe what these grievance

18 meetings involved?

19 A   Most of them were for attendance problems.

20 Q   And who would be at these meetings?

21 A   Well, usually the immediate supervisor, the foreman, the

22 person who was being accused of whatever, and then the union

23 steward.

24

25

1   Q   And generally when you attended these meetings did you

2   notice any kind of note taking by any of the -- by any

3   individual during those meetings?

4   A   No, not really. On occasion, like the steward -- I took

5   some notes, but I don't have any of my notes.

6   MR. RIVERA: Your Honor, may I approach the

7   witness?

8   Q   Mr. Luna, I'd like to show you what has been marked

9   Plaintiff's Exhibit No. 3, which by stipulation is offered

10   into evidence.

11   THE COURT: Admitted.

12   (Plaintiff's Exhibit No. 3 was received in evidence.)

13   Q   Do you recognize that document?

14   A   Well, not really, but I've seen the documents like this,

15   not this particular one.

16   Q   Okay. This document refers to -- well, why don't I let

17   you keep that. This document refers to Mr. Goluszek having

18   an injury for a year in 1983. Do you recall having a

19   conversation with Tony Goluszek regarding this letter?

20   A   No, I don't.

21   Q   The letter also refers to a safety program, and in the

22   second paragraph it starts out: "Our safety program". Were

23   you aware of any safety program that was at H.P. Smith?

24   A   Yes.

25   Q   Could you describe that program for us?

1   Q   January of what year?

2   A   '84.

3   Q   And do you remember --

4   A   That's the one with Ray Goytia, I think.

5   Q   And do you remember who was present during this?

6   A   That was Leo, Bill Clemente, Ray Goytia.

7   Q   Well, I'm talking about the time that you're talking

8   about with what Leo said. Who was present during that

9   conversation?

10   A   Leo, Bill, me and Tony.

11   Q   What did Mr. Karpinski say to you?

12   A   When we were talking out of the office he said that he

13   was getting to stick a six-shooter up Tony's ass to get him

14   to work faster.

15   Q   Did Tony Goluszek make any response?

16   A   He didn't, I don't think. He told me later to see what

17   he said, but not right away he didn't say nothing. When we

18   walked away he didn't say anything about it.

19   Q   Did he say anything to you later?

20   A   Yes, he said did you hear what he said? I said, yeah, I

21   heard him.

22   Q   Do you know how much later that was when you had that

23   conversation?

24   A   It was about five or ten minutes later, right when we

25   walked away.

1   we're going to file it a little late.

2   Q   But you have no recollection of that conversation

3   either, do you?

4   A   No.

5   Q   Okay. So you don't know whether a grievance was filed

6   on this or not, isn't that right?

7   A   Right.

8   Q   Now, if an employee doesn't file a grievance, then it's

9   appropriate for the company to treat this as a written

10   warning in his file, isn't that right?

11   A   Yes, I would imagine.

12   Q   Okay. And they can take future discipline based upon

13   this letter having been placed in the file and no grievance

14   filed with it, isn't that right?

15   A   Yes, sir.

16   Q   Pardon?

17   A   Yes, sir.

18   Q   Okay.

19   A   That's what the company is all about.

20   Q   Now, let me direct your attention to Exhibit 4.

21   A   I have it.

22   Q   Okay. Now, this particular grievance says: "Date of

23   grievance, 1-27-84, is that correct?

24   A   Right.

25   Q   Now, this would indicate that the grievance, the event

1   which created the grievance occurred on that date, isn't that

2   right?

3   A   Right.

4   Q   And what occurred on that date was the meeting with Ray

5   Goytia, Tony Goluszek, you and Mr. Clemente and you say Mr.

6   Karpinski was there.

7   A   Right.

8   Q   And this is the meeting where Mr. Karpinski made a

9   comment when he came away from the meeting about a

10 six-shooter?

11 A   Right.

12 Q   And at that meeting Mr. Goytia was very mad, wasn't he?

13 A   Yes.

14 Q   He felt that he was being picked on?

15 A   Right.

16 Q   And as I understand your recollection was Mr. Clemente

17 said, cool down, calm down, we've got to work together.

18 Let's go out and work and get it done, get the job done,

19 correct?

20 A   Right.

21 Q   Now, this written grievance is dated 2-7-84, is that

22 right?

23 A   Right.

24 Q   That means this written grievance as of 2-7-84, that's

25 Step 2, correct?

1   A   Right.

2   Q   So the first step was 1-26-84; the second step is

3   2-7-84, correct?

4   A   Right.

5   Q   You have to say yes or no.

6   A   I said right. Yes.

7   Q   Now, look at Exhibit No. 5. This is the letter denying

8   the grievance which is Exhibit No. 4, correct?

9   A   Yes, it is.

10   Q   And it says: "This grievance you first submitted for

11   Step 2 consideration on February 7th, 1984, and your own

12   statement, Step 1 was denied on January 26th." And so it's

13   denied as untimely, correct?

14   A   Right.

15   Q   Now, you had a right, did you not, as the union, and Mr.

16   Goluszek had the right, if you thought the time limit was

17   unfairly being called, to take this to the next step, didn't

18   you?

19   A   Yes.

20   Q   You didn't, isn't that right?

21   A   Well, we talked to Mr. Mietlicki after that.

22   Q   My question, Mr. Luna, you didn't take this grievance to

23   Step 3?

24   A   No, I didn't.

25   Q   And when he turned it down for being untimely you did

1   not pursue that to a higher level, is that correct?

2   A   Right. But you've got to understand, I mean you can't

3   pursue that much because the union wouldn't back you up. So

4   there was a lot of things that we never took to the third

5   step because, I mean, after a while it's just meaningless.

6   Q   Your testimony was no grievance -- time limits were

7   never called on grievances. That's your testimony, as I

8   understand it. But you're saying when this was turned down

9   for having a time limit called on it you didn't pursue it

10   because the union wouldn't support you, is that your

11   testimony?

12   A   Yes.

13   Q   Now, why wouldn't the union support you?

14   A   Because they're not going to come down for petty stuff

15   like this. I mean the company writes letters all the time

16   and you've got a thousand files of letters.

17   Q   My understanding of your testimony, Mr. Luna, is that

18   this grievance, which was filed on the 7th and turned down on

19   the 8th, that's the first time or the only time, I think you

20   said, the only time that you saw a grievance turned down that

21   quickly, is that right?

22   A   Right.

23   Q   Okay. Let me show you -- and by that quickly, you mean

24   turned down the next day?

25   A   Right. They gave us a letter dated the next day.

1   THE COURT: Oh, okay.

2   MR. GLADDEN: I hope.

3   BY MR. GLADDEN:

4   Q   Mr. Luna, going back to -- looking at 4 and 5 again.

5   When the company turned the grievance down as being untimely,

6   did Mr. Goluszek complain to you about that?

7   A   I don't recall.

8   Q   Did he accuse you of being negligent?

9   A   I don't think so, not that I recall.

10   Q   To your knowledge, did he file an unfair labor charge

11   saying you had been negligent in not pursuing his grievance?

12   A   Not that I know of.

13   Q   But he never complained to you, as far as you can

14   recall?

15   A   Right.

16   Q   Mr. Luna, did Mr. Goluszek ever bring Playboy magazines

17   himself to the plant?

18   A   Not that I can remember.

19   Q   Did he have them at the house when you shared a house

20   with him?

21   A   Not that I know of.

22   Q   You don't recall?

23   A   Not that I know of.

24   Q   Not that you know of. Your conversation with Mr.

25   Clemente, when you asked him for a written apology, that

1   occurred in his office; that was between you and him?

2   A   Right.

3   Q   And he said no, I'm not going to put it in writing; I

4   stand beside what I said?

5   A   Yes.

6   Q   Did he, in fact, orally apologize to Mr. Goluszek for

7   saying it was "shop talk"?

8   A   Yes.

9   Q   So before the grievance was even filed, Mr. Clemente had

10   orally apologized; he simply was not going to put the apology

11   in writing?

12   A   Right.

13   MR. GLADDEN: I have no further questions.

14   MR. RIVERA: We have no redirect.

15   THE COURT: All right. You're excused.

16

17   (END OF EXCERPT)

18

19

20

21

22

23

24

25

                    ANTHONY GOLUSZEK

<u>EXHIBIT 6</u>

<u>ANSWER TO INTERROGATORY NOs.
2, 3, 4, 5, 6, 8</u>

<u>December 1976</u>
     Operators at No. 2, 3, 4, 7, 14 Slitter machines on
night shift constant questions and statements to Plaintiff
as to why he is not married, why he has no girlfriend, and
that you have to be married to work here, etc. No oral
or written report was made.

<u>Winter 1977</u>
     Same operators to Plaintiff "If you can't fix the
machine, we'll have to call your daddy in" referring to
Foreman Mike Byczek, national origin - Polish. Plaintiff
reported to night supervisor Cal Adair. His response
was to later say the same things to Plaintiff in Spring
1978.

<u>Winter 1978</u>
     Night Supervisor, Cal Adair telling Plaintiff that
"if you can't fix the machine, it will be the sausage factor
for you," and that what Plaintiff needs is to "get married
and get some of that soft pink smelly stuff that's between
the legs of a woman." Plaintiff responded by asking Mr.
Adair not to comment about Plaintiff's personal life.

<u>Spring 1979</u>
     Operators at No. 3 and 7 Slitter machines on night
shift. Statements to Plaintiff that he should be married
and that he should go out with Kathy Kristein, employee
of Defendant - jeep driver. That "she would take good care"
of him. That "she fucks." Plaintiff reported this conduct
to Cal Adair. Mr. Adair's response was to later say to
Plaintiff that "if we can't get Tony to fix the machine
fast enough, we'll have to call in Kathy Kristein to fix
Tony.

<u>Winter 1981</u>
     After Plaintiff returned to night shift, Alan Corbert
said to Plaintiff "So you didn't get along with your daddy
on days? (reference to Mike Byczek) Did you get any pussy
anytime?" Soon thereafter Al Corbert and Willie Smith,
both machine operators would continuously ask the Plaintiff,
"Hey Tony, did you get any pussy today?" After asking Corbert
and Smith to not comment about his personal affairs, Plaintiff
reported this harassment to Bill Clemente. Clemente told
Plaintiff he would talk to Corbert and Smith.

<u>Spring 1982</u>
     Corbert again comments: "Hey Tony did you get fucked
yet. You better do something before your cock falls off"
Plaintiff told Corbert to "go to hell." Corbert on another
occasion comments: "Hey Tony did you get any black pussy
lately. You know when you get some black pussy you don't
come back. Corbert on another occasion calls Plaintiff
over to him to show him a nude woman in a Playboy Magazine,

and says: "Hey Tony come over here and check this out. Wouldn't you fuck her?" Plaintiff responded that he would. Plaintiff reported incidents to Bill Clemente and he said he would check it out.

Summer 1982

Corbert again says: "Hey Tony, you going to get any pussy this summer." Then Willie Smith says: "If you can Tony, try to get some black pussy this summer. It's black on the outside, but pink on the inside and just as good. Boy, you won't regret it. I guarantee it." Pliantiff responded by thanking Smith for the advice. Corbert, Smith and operators on No. 2, 3, 4, 6, and 7 slitter machines constant comments: "Hey Tondy look at this pussy. Wouldn't you like to fuck it in this position?" (Nude woman in the Playboy Magazine). "I bet there's women in H.P. Smith that are just as good? "Tony, when are you going to get fucked. Staying a virgin all your life is no fun. We're going to have to get you fucked. How about Kathy (jeep driver for Defendant)? No, Terry (Machine operator for Defendant)? No, Edna (jeep driver for Defendant)? She gives good blow jobs. You like blow jobs don't you Tony? I know you do. I got it. Wanda Jackson (machine operator for Defendant) on days. Perfect tits and fantastic ass. Boy, she would give you your money's worth. Hey, Tony how would you like sticking your nose up her.?" "Hey Tony, fuck that work and come over here and read these electrical drawings (actually they were Playboy Magazines). This will tell you how to fix it." Plaintiff responded that such conduct was a distraction, a waste of time, and adversely affecting his job performance. Plaintiff constantly asked that such conduct stop. Plaintiff reported to Bill Clemente of such conduct and that Playboy Magazines were being seen all over the plant. Clemente said he would do something.

Fall 1982

Al Corbert, stated to Plaintiff while standing with Willie Smith, Yevon Jerome (mechanic) and Fernando Ferandez (jeep operator): "Hey Tony, wouldn't you like to get your small cock in this shit (showing Plaintiff a picture of a nude woman from a Playboy Magazine)?" Smith then said: "Boy, I know Tony would jump right in. Look at him change colors on his face. He loves that shit." Then, Ferandez responds: "His (Plaintiff) cock couldn't handle it. He'd have to try it on me first. Jerome then states: "Tony never got into any boodie. Oh, you're not a man until you put your cock in your first ass and enjoy the shit and its smell." Plaintiff reported to Foreman Howie Strowshine of this incident. Plaintiff was told that since Cal Adair is Corbert's uncle nothing will happen on this, and that Plaintiff should forget about this. Plaintiff then made a report to Bill Clemente. Clemente told Plaintiff to forget about it, and that if he persisted with these complaints, he would be fired.

-2-

<u>Spring 1983</u>
     Al Corbert stated to Plaintiff: "Hey Tony did you
get any ass yet. You know those black girls got nice big
boodies. Plaintiff again reported to Bill Clemente, insisted
that something be done. Clemente responded that Plaintiff
would have to put up with it a little longer so that Clemente
could personally observe such conduct and fire those
responsible.

<u>May 27, 1983</u>
     Yvone Jerome asked Plaintiff, if he had ever had put
his "dick in a women's ass" and would Plaintiff allow some
men to do the same to him. Plaintiff responded that "You
know a lot of people would kill a person for saying that."
Jerome then said that he was a Vietnam Vet, and could kill
Plaintiff with a piano wire. Plaintiff responded: "Well,
why don't you take a swing, and see how far you can go.
I bet when I deck you you'll fall to pieces.

<u>Summer 1983</u>
     Fernando Ferandez stated to Plaintiff that he wanted
to go "bisexual" with Plaintiff. Plaintiff responded that
"the only way you will go with one is with your teeth knocked
out." Ferandez responded that he enjoyed SM. Plaintiff
responded: "You're helpless. Yevone Jerome asked Plaintiff
if he had ever raped a women or a little girl. Plaintiff
responded "No have you?" Plaintiff reported these incidents
to Bill Clemente. He stated that he would handle it.

<u>Fall 1983</u>
     Yvone Jerome accused Plaintiff and Tony Luna of being
gay, because at one time, Plaintiff and Luna had shared
an apartment. Plaintiff told Jerome to "get out of here
before I puty you away. Plaintiff reported this to Bill
Clemente and Tony Luna. Luna told Plaintiff that there
was little he could do, that others were complaining of
the same thing, but that nothing is being done about it.

<u>Winter 1983</u>
     Al Corbert came up behind Plaintiff with a stick and
stuck it up Plaintiff's back side while yelling boodie,
boodie man, and then ran off. Plaintiff reported this to
Bill Clemente stating that he can not take this harassment
much longer. Clemente stated that "don't worry, you won't
be here much longer." Plaintiff reported to Luna and Luna
told him that he was aware of the problem, that others were
also complaining, and that he would pursue the matter.

<u>January 1984</u>
     Yevone Jerome told Plaintiff he was going to "hypnotize"
him to be a "boodie man. Al Corbert again came up from
behind Plaintiff repeating his earlier conduct with a stick
while yelling boodie, boodie, boodie man, and then ran off.

-3-

August 29, 1983
Tony Luna (union steward) stated to Plaintiff" "How come my dog is pregnant; did you knock her up?" Plaintiff responded: "Tony, how would you like it if I said that to you about your old lady?" Luna responded that he would beat Plaintiff up. Plaintiff responded that that was the way he felt about what Luna said.

January 26, 1984
At a meeting with Bill Clemente, Roy Goytia, Tony Luna, and Plaintiff among others Goytia complained to Clemente that Plaintiff was harassing him. Plaintiff told Clemente of all the harassment he has continually faced. Clemente responded that "Well Tony, in your case fucking ass about another person is just plain shop talk." Plaintiff and Luna disagreed. After the meeting, Plaintiff and Luna decided that if nothing was done in a few days, they would file a grievance.

February 1984
Plaintiff asked for a meeting with Jim Rooney, Vice-President, regarding the sexual harassment. No meeting ever occurred Plaintiff's grievance was denied review due to missing a time limitation. Plaintiff appealed decision, but nothing further was heard.

Leo Karpinski, while in the Slitter Office with Plaintiff and Wanda Johnson, asked Plaintiff how he would like to have a date with Ms. Johnson. Karpinski then asked Ms. Johnson if she would go out with Plaintiff. Ms. Johnson left the office. At nother time, Karpenski told Plaintiff that he should get a "six-shooter up your ass."

March 1984
Yevone Jerome told Plaintiff that "I hear you turned your boss in for talking about ass sex. You know you like it." Plaintiff asked to be left alone.
Willie Smith told Plaintiff that he should not have compalined about this "ass sex" since "a little shit on your dick never hurt any body." Bill Clemente called Plaintiff over to No. 14 machine and asked why it wasn't fixed faster, and that the problem with the machine is Plaintiff's breathing. Plaintiff suggested that maybe Clemente could remedy his breathing by stepping outside with Plaintiff.

April 1, 1984
Bill Clemente told Plaintiff that Tony Luna was terminated for wastage of time, and that Plaintiff was only supposed to deal with the other shop stewards, Joe Greenwald and Roger Young. Plaintiff did contact Greenwald and Young about his grievance, and they told him that it was a "dead issue."

April 1984
Roy Goytia told Plaintiff that he was going to be fired

 ANTHONY GOLUSZEK

soon. That the company has friends in Government, the police
force and so on, and that Plaintiff did not know who he
was dealing with. Willie Smith told Plaintiff that he was
"hot today" and that maybe "he was going to get a fuck from
Edna Rangel (an employee of defendant) today".

May 1984
        Bill Clemente Told Plaintiff that he was a bad apple
that was going to get weeded out. Leo Karpinski told
Plaintiff that after Plaintiff was fired from Defendant's
employment, he would be very luck to find another job and
that Plaintiff didn't need a job because he doesn't "fuck
anyway".

                                    ANTHONY GOLUSZEK

-5-

TINLEY

S. Criminal
Court

S. = Supreme

4/2/07 Anthony Goluszek

you got till 6/2/07

SUPREME COURT OF THE UNITED STATES
OFFICE OF THE CLERK
WASHINGTON, DC 20543-0001

April 16, 2007

Anthony P. Goluszek
3034 Chgo Road, Apt. 7
S. Chicago, IL 60411

    RE: Anthony P. Goluszek

Dear Mr. Goluszek:

In reply to your letter or submission, received April 10, 2007, I regret to inform you that the Court is unable to assist you in the matter you present.

Under Article III of the Constitution, the jurisdiction of this Court extends only to the consideration of cases or controversies properly brought before it from lower courts in accordance with federal law and filed pursuant to the Rules of this Court.

Your papers are herewith returned.

                Sincerely,
                William K. Suter, Clerk
                By:
                Clayton R. Higgins, Jr.
                (202) 479-3019

Enclosures

Since the following was endorsement of sexual harassment by labor
board grievance was a non gross
level by Crawford in 1984.

In 1989 Federal district court
86C8412 and 7th circuit appeal
Thomas F Strup Clerk and judges
Posner, Flaum and Ripple, Fraud
assult and harassment was endorsed.

In 1992 Sargent Folliard Chicago
Police not a criminal matter was
endorsed too.

Supreme court clerk Higgins
signed also recieved papers of case
believed not to be a criminal
matter too.

What was said, you can use
at work, bars parks and etc. for
harassment of persons and assult

of person by poking of.

If arrested place bond as soon as possible. Goto a gay jury in a criminal court to present papers to get off.

Then goto civil court for mental damages of being arrested. Get cash award for pain and suffering.

www.ingramcontent.com/pod-product-compliance
Lightning Source LLC
Chambersburg PA
CBHW021657070726
47591CB00017B/642